Peaks & Pitfalls

7 Best Practices and Pitfalls of Professional Development
Includes excerpts from participants, sample schedules, and
thought-provoking evaluation/accountability forms designed to
foster optimal learning environments; thus transformations.

by
Dr. Arnita Rena Hall

Opulence PUBLISHING

Cumming, Georgia

Peaks and Pitfalls
by Arnita Rena Hall
ISBN 978-0-9964717-0-1
Copyright © 2015 by Arnita Rena Hall

Published by Opulence Publishing
1595 Peachtree Pwky Ste. 204-218
Cumming, GA 30041

Printed in the United States of America. All rights reserved. No part of this document may be reproduced or transmitted in any form, by any means (electronic, photocopying, recording, or otherwise) without the written permission of the author.

Table of Contents

PREFACE	viii
Introduction	10
Core Elements of Professional Development	16
Definition vs. Understanding	
Goals and Objectives	
High Quality, Robust, and Stimulating	
SEVEN PEAKS	
1. Brain Compatibility	27
2. Structure and Preparedness	37
3. Delivery Methods	54
4. Motivate and Inspire	79
5. Challenge and Engage	87
6. Accountability and Evaluation	96
7. Stimulating Environment	105
SEVEN PITFALLS	
Introduction to Pitfalls	125
1. Planning and Preparation	128
2. Change	135
3. Delivery Methods	142
4. Learning Materials, Resources & Terminology	151
5. Unrealistic Expectations	159
6. Empty Vessels	166
7. Implementation Dip	172
APPENDICES	
Appendix A Examples of Sample Schedules	180
Appendix B Implementation Items to Ponder When Crafting Optimal-Learning Goals and Objectives	195
Appendix C Evaluation Form	197
Appendix D Sample Note-taking Form (Four "As" Protocol)	216
Appendix E Professional Development Quotes	217
Appendix F Innovative Approaches to Sustain Professional Development Offerings	218
TESTIMONIES	

To my Prince (Kent), your love and support over the years and throughout the crafting of this book has been unwavering. You are integral to my success and I will forever be grateful.

Love,
Your Princess, Rena

Acknowledgements

Acknowledgments are forwarded first and foremost to my family and friends (Kent, Kenny, and Jonathan, you all are my rock and the center of my life). Thanks for your continued love and support. Mommy, your constant inspirations are key to my success; I'm proud to be your daughter.

To the stakeholders within the RTS program, supported by UWMN. Your communications and interactions with me served as inspirations and key motivators for this book. It is my dream that others will be able to prosper as you all have, and that they will educate in the true fashion of "always putting the students and their needs first."

I could not complete this page without acknowledging and giving thanks to my Lord and Savior, Jesus Christ. Because of Him, I am where I am, and I am able to bless others via this book.

The days of teacher-staff development sessions consisting of "sit-and-get" workshops and expert-delivered awareness campaigns are long gone. We are now moving toward more effective and more engaging professional development models. Research and experience help us recognize that high-quality ongoing professional development that deepens teachers' content knowledge and pedagogical skills provides opportunities for practice, research, and reflection, and includes efforts that are job-embedded, sustained, and collaborative and will assist in the goal to remain up-to-date (Sparks, 2002).

Preface

The work of improving teacher training and support still pose as a key element of any educational improvement plan. Effective teaching is an activity that can be learned; and the notion that someone is born to teach is simply inaccurate.

For the past twenty years, Dr. Hall has been engaged in a myriad; of professional development opportunities, stemming the gamut of sessions from small learning community groups to reaching departments and organizations of five hundred plus, and reaching audiences far and wide via collaborations and consultations with organizations in various countries and municipalities. Of these opportunities a few consistent threads continue to present. These are facilitators' preparedness, session content, experiential engagement, the environment of the training, and the methods in which the training is delivered.

Dr. Hall's daily roles and responsibilities have dictated allegiance to professional development as she oversees the professional development of more than one hundred early childhood education teachers and their assistants. While this may seem like a small feat, it is truly a huge offering as early childhood educators are trusted with ensuring our nation's children are prepared to learn and are equipped with the skills necessary to do so. Therefore, they along with parents/caretakers are optimal in the process of developing a solid educational foundation on which children in their care will prosper.

Teachers, therefore, must always be prepared, eager, motivated, and inspiring, as well as consistently engaged! To master the task of preparing our youngest children to achieve, educational organizations, departments, and societies must prepare teachers in a manner in which they are respected, are able to process training information, demonstrate continuous growth, and have the ability to engage with their colleagues as to best practices, optimal learning conditions, and expectations and avenues of support for both their students and themselves.

This book is being written to aid early education directors, program managers, conference/event organizers, and school systems with the tools necessary to take their professional development offerings to the next level, by incorporating the Seven Peaks (Best Practices) of Highly Successful Professional Development Offerings and avoiding Seven Easy to Overlook Pitfalls of Professional Development Trainings. The steps provided are simple to implement but will yield profound results, allowing you to hold your team accountable in a nurturing and supportive manner.

Introduction

Let's face it. professional development, as we have known it for years now, has yielded little or no positive effects on student learning. Thus complain the many weary professionals who flinch at the mere mention of the word "workshop." In the collective imagination, the term "professional development day" conjures only images of coffee breaks, consultants in elegant outfits, and schools barren of kids.

Of course, professional development was never intended to trigger such pessimistic reactions. Even critics of the professional development movement admit that all forms of teacher development, whether effective or not, have at their core the noble intention of improving student learning. We might disagree with the implementation processes available, but not with their purpose. Indeed, when correctly implemented, professional development actually yields the results intended. In this era of high-stakes testing and increased accountability, it is necessary to reposition professional development so the collective efforts of teachers, students, and administrators result in enhanced learning for all members of the teaching community.

This book is designed to produce and encourage the implementation of optimal learning within a professional development environment. As you will uncover via the chapters presented, professional development is interwoven into the fabrics of one's profession. The goals of professional development are varied and should include opportunities that allow participants to expand their knowledge base via the acquisition of new information or through sessions where additional theories, content, or concepts are being introduced as to the best practices or new techniques relevant to their positions. Additionally, quality professional development should offer opportunities of personal reflection and self-evaluation as to one's current roles and responsibilities and their relevance to the topic being covered.

Lastly, the book is grounded in brain development and the manners in which adults learn. This is critical, as professional development must be delivered in a manner in which the individual is able to process the information, thus transforming the content into practice via the travel from short-term memory to long-term.

This book presents the aforementioned items and expands on these to ensure professional development is not an afterthought but key to the organization's ability to develop and consistently provides a platform for staff as they continue to craft and implement best practices.

I have chosen to narrow my focus as to the severity of professional development. Indeed there are more than seven peaks (best practices) and seven pitfalls administrators and planners should be mindful. Seven was chosen as an identifiable number as it signifies greatness and strength, which is the epitome of professional development embodiment.

The number seven is synonymous with several great and powerful things, including the continents, the days of the week, the manner in which the brain takes in and manipulates information, the wonders of the world, virtues, deadly sins, and mischief and indulgences alike. There are seven colors in the rainbow, seven continents, and the fact that the moon changes phases every seven days. According to many faiths, seven is displayed time and time again as it symbolizes God's holiness, perfection, and sovereignty. There are seven heavens and seven heavenly bodies. And for my musical friends, there are seven musical notes represented on the diatonic scale, which are stated as being the most pleasing to the ear (Denver, 2011).

Further exploration of the number seven also reveals its significance in literature and science as seen in Grimm's Fairytales' Snow White and the Seven Dwarfs and The Seven Ravens; and the number of rows of the periodic table is seven (correlation to the manner in which information is processed).

Personally, I was driven and connected to the number seven as I am the seventh child of my parents; my address reflects the number seven; and I have always listed or referred to items in chunks of seven. (Back then I did not know the real significant of the number seven). If you ask my mom and probably my husband, they would both agree that oftentimes I am asked to do things seven times prior to them being completed; or as my mom would definitely vouch, it took me seven times to get it right.

What I came to understand as I studied is when one's environment changes, it takes the brain seven seconds to assimilate to its new environment. Therefore, I am happy to report, I was not just playing or goofing off when asked to comply. I was simply giving my brain the time it needed to process so I could complete the request appropriately. We each learn in various manners, hence Gardner's Theory on Multiple Intelligence. This leads me to believe the manner in which items were requested or introduced to me was not one that initially aligned with my learning style(s) and preference(s); therefore, understanding and mastery took a little longer for me to obtain.

Seven is more than a number in which I aligned this book. As Aristotle points out, "All human actions have one or more of these seven causes: chance, nature, compulsion, habit, reason, desire, and passion." My goal in highlighting the number seven is to highlight and easily associate the manner in which the brain processes information; our ability to transfer the information obtained from short-term to long-term memory; and mostly importantly the ability to translate the information into practice, which if practiced for twenty-one straight days (three weeks; product of seven) becomes habit.

When connecting the topic of professional development to the powers of seven, it seemed fitting that I synthesize my experience and associate it with the seven most important best practices and pitfalls I have discovered over the years from facilitating trainings, researching, engaging in the professional development offerings/trainings, serving as an educational consultant, and through attendance/participation in PD sessions.

A "peak" (best practice) can be defined as a technique or methodology that, through experience and research, has proven to reliably lead to a desired result. A commitment to using best practice in any field is a commitment to assembling one's knowledge and technology to ensure success. Best practice is used frequently in the fields of health care, government administration, the education system, project management, and hardware and software product development (Rouse, 2014). A best practice tends to spread throughout a field or industry after a success has been demonstrated. However, it is often noted that demonstrated best practices can be slow to spread, even within an organization. According to the American Productivity and Quality Center, the three main barriers to adoption of a best practice are a lack of knowledge about current best practices, a lack of motivation to make changes involved in their adoption, and a lack of knowledge and skills required to make learning transformative (Strahl, 2015).

Pitfalls Pitfalls are those pesky duties, tasks, or obligations we often take for granted and seem to over look, yet ones others seem to seize upon. Pitfalls can be associated with hidden or unsuspected danger or difficulty. In the professional development arena these are bountiful as it is impossible to orchestrate a training to meet the needs of all attendees. However, the seven chapters in the book associated with pitfalls are ones that seem to be common and often associated with the reasons as to why the sessions/training offered were not received well, implemented, or evaluated. After planning, facilitating, or consulting on roughly one thousand professional development sessions, the pitfalls included here are ones educators list on average as being negligent in the training environment, viewed as critical to success, and ones discussed time and time again by myself at consultations, implementations, and during evaluations/reflective opportunities.

After reading this book, your charge is to seize upon the seven peaks and never again commit the pitfalls. I believe when we know better we do better. Since you have taken the first step of reading this book, you are expanding your knowledge, thus you are agreeing to implement these practices (remember, there are only seven) as you commit to doing BETTER! *Caution! The results will be TRANSFORMATIVE.*

Reflective Notes

Think about your professional development offerings and schedules. Are these aligned more with those identified as peaks or pitfalls?

1.
2.
3.
4.
5.
6.
7.

Additional items I want to remember from the Introduction:

_____
_____
_____
_____
_____
_____
_____
_____
_____

The best teachers are the ones who are struggling to become more than they are, on any given day, and who demonstrate to their students that this quest to learn and to grow, to accept failure, and go on to new challenges, is what life is all about (Gordon, 2004).

Introduction

Core Elements of Professional Development
Definition vs. Understanding
Goals and Objectives
High Quality, Robust, and Stimulating

Definition vs. Understanding

Every teacher can probably describe a boring or downright ineffective professional development (PD) experience they've encountered. In fact, one out of three professional development experiences can be categorized as ineffective. There are many challenges when trying to design a successful and engaging professional development program for continuous teacher education. Whether you're an administrator looking for useful tips or an educator who wants to hone your own skills, the research-based tips embedded will help you avoid some of the most common problems and mistakes made in professional development training and incorporate only cutting-edge techniques.

To ensure goal attainment for the optimal PD training program, cross-referencing of data yields many definitions of professional development and various elements associated with each. I have synthesized these to the following:

Professional development is the continuous process of improving and increasing capabilities of staff through access to education and training opportunities—internal and external—to the outside organization or by watching others perform the job (coaching/mentoring). Other facets of PD are implemented through informal contexts such as discussions among work colleagues, independent reading/research, observations of a colleague's work, or other learning from a peer, in addition to the fostering of professional learning communities.

Continuous professional development helps build and maintain morale of staff members and is thought to attract high-quality staff to an organization. PD is established and vetted through administrators, yet becomes profound and enforced by administrators' modeling and commitment to the process. Effective PD addresses the core areas of teaching—content, curriculum, assessment, and instruction. Regardless of duration and the type of PD, each offering should address teacher and student needs through approaches that are appropriate for conditions in their respective school/early education environment. These offerings should be long-term, ongoing, sequenced, and cumulative, providing teachers opportunities to gain new knowledge and skills, reflect on changes in their teaching practices, and increase their capacities over time.

Professional development can bring out the best in schools/centers and organizations and create a culture of collaboration, mutual respect, and shared accountability. This becomes a culture in which participants' voices are heard; and when they are included in the decision-making session they feel a greater sense of ownership of organizational/school achievement. The more supportive the culture, the stronger the effectiveness of the professional development activity. Trust is especially important during times of change, and since increased professional development represents a significant change in organizations, attention must be paid to building and maintaining trust throughout the collaboration so professional development can flourish (Farina, 2014).

Goals and Objectives

The objectives of professional development are to help employees enhance their job skills, obtain job-related knowledge and information, increase productivity and efficiency, and/or prepare for higher-level positions. Professional development activities may include, but are not limited to, workshops, seminars, teleconferences, credit and non-credit college courses (traditional or online), allegiance to professional learning communities, and audio-visual materials as deemed necessary and appropriate for the target audience.

As in all professions, but especially for educators, it can take years to gain the skills needed to be effective in their roles. The complexity of teaching is so great that one-third of teachers leave the profession within three years and 50 percent leave within five years (Ingersoll, 2003). Even experienced teachers confront great challenges each year, including changes in subject content, new instructional methods, advances in technology, new laws and procedures, and student learning needs. In the early education arena this complexity is manifested in state law changes, the defining of early education, the state's quality rating scale, and the evolving research on brain development, each leading to the incorporation of differentiated instruction.

Educators who do not experience effective professional development trainings do not improve their skills and student learning suffers. A conversation with Commissioner Huffman of the Tennessee Department of Education revealed that "having an ill-prepared or improperly trained teacher is worse for students as the impact stifles their learning and negates their trajectory for success over the span of five years."

Daily, educators juggle an overwhelming number of unfamiliar issues, such as classroom management, instruction, curriculum, school culture and operations, test preparation and administration, state standards, parent relations, and interactions with other teachers/personnel. Left to themselves, teachers/administrators may develop counterproductive behaviors. With extra support, however, teachers (the novice and experts) learn more effective practices to apply to daily challenges. Additional support also helps schools retain new teachers and establishes a successful roadmap of skills needed to become effective educators. Most importantly, research shows that teachers who received intensive peer-to-peer mentoring and professional development training had a significant effect on student achievement after as little as two years (Gulamhussein, 2013).

HIGH QUALITY, ROBUST, AND STIMULATING

Just how critical is professional learning for teachers to educational improvement? In many ways professional development is the link between the design and implementation of education reform and the ultimate success of reform efforts in schools. The evaluation of educator effectiveness based on student test scores and classroom observation, for example, has the potential to drive instructional improvement and promises to reveal important aspects of classroom performance and success. That information may, in some cases, be used as the basis for critical personnel decisions such as whether to dismiss an educator or increase his or her salary. Yet to have the impact on student learning that supporters of reform intend, evaluation needs to be accompanied by insightful feedback about teacher performance that leads to a strategic set of professional-learning activities to help educators improve their practice.

High-quality, robust, and stimulating professional development are ones educators and staff in general hope to receive. When sessions are planned with these components, the win for both the organization and employee are met and staff leave with a feeling of accomplishment, time well spent, and ideas, strategies and techniques they can then go back into their daily practices and employ immediately.

High Quality Professional Development (HQPD) is a set of coherent learning experiences that is systematic, purposeful, and structured over a sustained period of time with the goal of improving teacher practice and student outcomes. It enables educators to facilitate the learning of students by acquiring and applying knowledge, skills, and abilities that address student needs and goals of the district, school, child development/educational centers, and individuals.

Oftentimes when quality is referenced, our minds are easily transformed to that of the "best of the best." When speaking of cars, this may reflect on models such as Land Rovers, Mercedes, Audis, and Cadillacs. When food is considered, quality is reflective in a decadent cake, a juicy lobster, or a tender steak. Quality when referring to professional development High Quality is revealed through many facets such as facilitator preparedness, the engagement of the executive function of the brain, adherence to agendas, one's ability to relate the topic to that of their current roles and responsibilities, meeting the stated goals and objectives, and the pace as to the day in correlation with the knowledge provided. When all of these facets are employed in tandem the results are groundbreaking, thus transformative, as learning is presented in various forms and fashions to not only garner the executive functioning of the brain but concepts easily adopted into daily and consistent practice.

High-quality professional development includes several interrelated factors and should be based on substantive, well-defined objectives. It implies rich content specifically chosen to deepen and broaden the knowledge and skills of teachers, educational assistants, principals, administrators, paraprofessionals, and other key education staff. At the forefront of HQPD development are structures, reflecting well-thought-out delivery; efficient use of time; varied and effective styles of pedagogy; discourse and application; and 'the use of formative and summative assessment to promote understanding. Creating high-quality professional development opportunities demands the guidance of experienced educators and other professionals who have a thorough and up-to-date understanding of the content themselves and who can fully engage participants in the desired learning concepts.

High-quality professional development should:

a. Improve and increase teachers' knowledge of the subjects they teach, and enable teachers to become highly qualified;

   First and foremost, teachers must have a deep and broad understanding of the discipline(s) they teach. In planning and targeting professional development experiences, primary emphasis should be placed on providing a continuum of learning experiences that are clearly focused on building content knowledge.

b. Be sustained, intensive, and classroom focused in order to have a positive and lasting impact on classroom instruction and teachers' performance in the classroom;

   The total duration of the experience should involve a significant investment of time to meet the learning objectives of a substantive professional development program. The professional development activity does not need to occur as one contiguous section of time, but the continuum should be articulated. Sustained professional development often includes both preparatory activities, such as independent reading, and follow-up sessions that allow teachers to discuss and critique their application of new learning.

   Intensive professional development is characterized by continuous, rigorous, and concentrated learning activities. Intensive professional development should involve participants in an innovative, multidimensional learning experience. Complex experiences, including problem solving, issue analysis, research, and systematic investigation, should be a core component of the overall program. Likewise, the RIGOR of the activity should demand more of participants than simple comprehension of the concepts presented. It is best practices that teachers immediately have the opportunity to engage in skill application after concept introduction and review. Activities should be interrelated, sequential, and build toward an ultimate outcome.

The content of any professional development activity must relate back to the classroom and have application to student learning and success. For example, professional development should focus on such things as strategies for improving student academic achievement, improving classroom management, or developing ways teachers may work more effectively with parents to improve student achievement.

c. Aligned with, and directly related to one's states/accreditation body or local standards;

Ensuring student achievement of your state's academic standards is the primary goal of pre-K-12 instruction, and professional development should distinctly promote teachers' fluency with the concepts, skills, and processes embedded within the standards. Professional development should relate directly to the state's academic standards and the curriculum framework in concert with the identified needs of teachers.

d. Be structured on scientifically based research demonstrated to improve student academic achievement or substantially increase the knowledge and teaching skills of teachers.

Professional development activities should provide teachers with the opportunity to learn effective instructional strategies that are based on research. Generally, this includes strategies that have undergone a rigorous, objective, and systematic review; were evaluated using reproducible experiential or quasi-experiential designs; and were peer reviewed.

e. Be sponsored by school divisions, colleges, universities, organizations, associations, or other entities experienced in providing professional development activities to teachers and instructors;

f. Be delivered by individuals who have demonstrated qualifications and credentials in the focus area of the professional development;

g. Support the success of all learners including children with special needs and limited English proficiency;

Ensuring the success of all students, regardless of disability, language proficiency, or socio-economic status is a crucial goal for educational institutions.

h. Provide training for teachers in the use of technology so that technology and technology applications are effectively used in the classroom to improve teaching and learning in the curricula and other educational domains;

i. Promote the use of data and assessments to improve instruction; and

j. Be reviewed for high quality and evaluated after completion to determine if the intended results were achieved.

To have a positive and lasting impact on classroom instruction and teacher performance in the classroom, professional development should be focused on the results it is intended to produce.

Reflective Notes

How are your proposed activities reflecting and aligning to participant effort beyond attendance?

1.
2.
3.
4.
5.
6.
7.

Additional items I want to remember or incorporate are:

_____
_____
_____
_____
_____
_____
_____
_____
_____

The ideal professional development experience as described by teachers are:

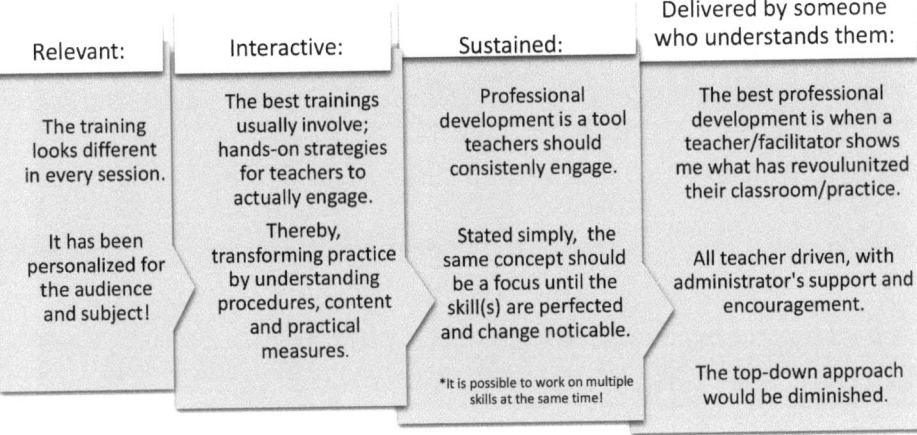

Seven Peaks

Educators who do not experience effective professional development do not improve their skills, and student learning suffers.

CHAPTER 1

Brain Compatibility

In the brain, the ability to hold on to and work with information, focus thinking, filter distractions, and switch gears is like an airport having a highly effective air traffic control system to manage the arrivals and departures of dozens of planes on multiple runways. Scientists refer to these capacities as executive function and self-regulation—a set of skills that relies on three types of brain function: working memory, mental flexibility, and self-control.

Think of those times you've left a professional development workshop saying to yourself, "Wow, that really made me think!" Now think of those grimmer occasions when you said, "What a waste of time! I'd have preferred a root canal." Why did you learn in one situation but not in the other? During my tenure as an educator and educational consultant, I have witnessed professional development delivered in many formats. However, the goal of all was to offer teachers and administrators something new that would enhance their effectiveness. Yet, enhancement happens only if participants actually acquire knowledge/skills, which raises the questions: As teachers participate in learning activities, how do their brains determine what—if anything—to take away? And how can we use the brain's ability to process and decipher to improve learning activities for teachers?

How we feel about a learning situation often affects attention and memory more quickly than what we think about it. Adults come to a learning activity with strong emotions. But a fully developed prefrontal cortex enables most adults to consciously dampen their emotions. If the activity captures an adult learner's interest, the mature cortex will override any negative feelings, and learning will occur. But teachers who are deeply annoyed by mandatory attendance or who feel emotionally detached may resist learning. Participants can conceal their negative feelings, but they may surreptitiously turn to activities like doodling unless the activity is engaging enough to connect to positive emotion.

When people feel positive about a learning situation, chemicals called endorphins and dopamine become active. Endorphins provide a feeling of euphoria. Dopamine stimulates the prefrontal cortex, keeping the individual attentive, interactive, and likely to remember what he or she experienced. Negative feelings, on the other hand, cause the hormone cortisol to enter the bloodstream. Cortisol puts the brain into survival mode. This shifts the brain's attention away from learning so it can deal with the source of stress. Instead of learning, the brain remembers the pressure and registers these kinds of situations as unpleasant.

Professional development leaders should ask themselves the following questions to determine whether the format and content of their programs connect to positive emotions in most teachers and avoid triggering negative ones:

- Does the program offer learning experiences associated with moderate challenge, excitement, creativity, and joy so teachers will be more likely to remember what they learn and implement it in the upcoming weeks?

- Does the program speak to a problem that teachers identified rather than some outside entity? If not, can you connect this content to teachers' concerns?

- Have you included opportunities for experiential learning and activities that address a variety of learning styles?

- Will participants give leaders regular feedback on the trainings—and receive regular feedback?

The process of professional development should also be based on sound educational practice such as contextual teaching. Contextual teaching presents information in familiar contexts and in contexts in which the information is useful. It is effective because it takes advantage of the fact that learning occurs best when learners process new information or knowledge in such a way that it makes sense to them in their own frames of reference. Contextual teaching is consistent with the way the mind naturally functions, as articulated, for example, in Caine, Caine, and Crowell's (1999) twelve principles of brain-based learning:

- The brain is a living system—a collection of parts that function as a whole.
- The brain/mind is social.
- The search for meaning is innate.
- The search for meaning occurs through patterning.
- Emotions are critical for patterning.
- Every brain simultaneously perceives and creates wholes and parts.
- Learning involves both focused attention and peripheral perception.
- Learning always involves conscious and unconscious processes.

- There are at least two ways of organizing memory.

- Learning is developmental.

- Complex learning is enhanced by challenge and inhibited by threat associated with a sense of helplessness or fatigue.

- Every brain is uniquely organized.

Past experiences refers to experiences the brain encodes into long-term memory and readily recalls. Past experiences always affect new learning. As we learn something new, our brain transfers into working memory any long-stored items it perceives as related to the new information. These items interact with new learning to help us interpret information and extract meaning, which is part of the principle called transfer (Sousa, 2006).

This process affects whether a teacher will be disposed to commit to a new professional initiative. If that teacher's brain recalls that previous professional development activities were worthwhile, then he or she will approach a new activity positively. Conversely, if the teacher's brain rejected past professional development activities as meaningless, that teacher will likely come to the new activity with little motivation. In this situation, convincing the brain that attending to new information will prove useful for the future becomes the major—and daunting—task for professional development leaders.

Adults attach meaning to new learning by drawing on a multitude of past experiences, but they may not find a match that makes it relevant. When a participant in a professional development activity asks, "Why do I need to know this?" that individual is neither readily connecting the day's training session of learning to past teaching experiences nor accepting it as meaningful. To create experiences participants perceive as meaningful, professional development leaders should:

- Directly connect the new initiative to job-related goals. For example, activities that demonstrate precisely how the teachers use new strategies to help students learn literacy concepts are more valuable than general suggestions.

- Present the topic over enough time and in enough depth so teachers gain a thorough understanding of how it relates to their work. It is foolish, for instance, to expect participants to make in-depth connections in a one-hour workshop, especially if there are no follow-up activities.

- Use instructional modalities other than "telling." Participants need to see the strategy modeled and then apply it themselves soon thereafter. When teachers actively participate in a demonstration of the primacy/recency effect, for example, they more clearly recognize that the brain remembers best the first and last items presented in a learning episode—and they are more likely to sequence instruction with this phenomenon in mind.

- Initiate actionable research. Conducting actionable research in the classroom enables teachers to personally assess the effectiveness of a new strategy, obtain validation for incorporating new strategies into their repertoire, and investigate specific problems that affect their teaching.

- Promote in-school study groups around the topic. As group members exchange new research and share in-class experiences, they can analyze why—and under what conditions—a strategy is effective. Participating in study groups helps teachers who are reluctant to try out new ideas gain confidence.

Learning Implications and the Brain

1. The brain is a PATTERN SEEKER, made up of a network of neurons that provide the structure for individual neural maps of meaning. The brain is constantly on the alert for patterns as it processes and stores new information.	1. Learning experiences must MAKE SENSE to allow new information to settle securely into existing brain patterns of knowledge. New learning experiences should facilitate connections to prior understandings and experiences, and should be meaningful to students.
2. Although the number of neurons in the brain cannot increase, the network of CONNECTIONS between neurons can increase in number and alter physically to be more efficient. These changes have been shown to happen: * in stimulating and enriching environments *through active mental and physical engagement with materials	2. LEARNING ENVIRONMENTS should be: * sensually stimulating * supplied with a variety of learning materials * encouraging of active engagement with materials * supportive of discourse and exchange between participants *Continuation on next page*

3. The brain inputs information through the SENSES passing from the brainstem through the limbic system (the emotional control center) and then on to the neo-cortex. Emotions are at the base of all learning.	3. Teachers must attend to the EMOTIONAL ASPECTS of learning. The learning environment must be emotionally and physically safe.
4. The brain can cognitively process and pay conscious ATTENTION to only one thing at a time.	4. Participants need TRAINING to develop successful attention habits: HOW to focus attention and WHAT to attend to. Facilitators cannot assume participants have these abilities. These skills must be fostered and nourished.
5. The brain requires TIME to build and enhance the physical connections that are necessary to process input and transfer information from short-term memory to permanent long-term memory.	5. A PD training must provide for REST and REFLECTION, time to think, process, reflect, and relax.
6. EVERY BRAIN IS UNIQUE. Each brain is made up of its own unique genetic material and develops at its own individual pace. Each individual person has a collection of life experiences that are different from every person.	6. EVERY PARTICIPANT IS UNIQUE. Facilitators should try to understand, celebrate, and challenge the individuality of their participants. Participants should not be made to conform to facilitators' agendas. Educational programs should be structured to meet individual participants' needs and abilities whenever this is possible.

To fully engage the brain through presentations, the most effective presentation must move back and forth through interrelated neural systems, weaving them together. These areas are interconnected under usual circumstances, like a complete "workout" in the gym where one can rotate from one station to another. Similarly, in teaching, it is most effective to work one neural area and then move on to another. Facilitators should engage facilitators with a story/summary to provide the context. Make sure this vignette can touch the emotional parts of participants' brains. This will activate and prepare the cognitive parts of the brain for storing information.

Information is easiest to digest when there is emotional "seasoning"—humor, empathy, sadness, and fear all make "dry" facts easier to swallow. Give a fact or two; link these facts into related concepts. Move back to the narrative to help participants make the connection between the concept and the story. Go back to another fact. Reinforce the concepts. Facilitators should reconnect with the original story. In and out, bob and weave, among facts, concept, and narrative to ensure learning and appeal to the senses as well as to cognition.

While this seems like a strange sequence of events for adult learners, it's imperative to remember that human beings are storytelling primates. We are curious, and we love to learn. The challenge for each facilitator is to find ways to engage participants and take advantage of the novelty-seeking property of the human brain to facilitate learning.

Anatomy and Functional Areas of the Brain

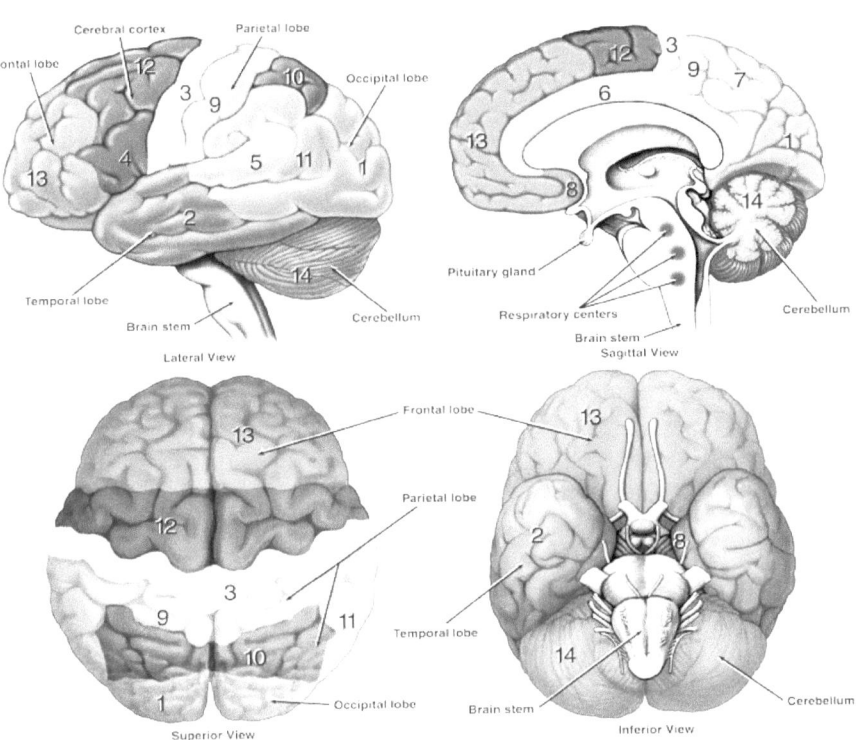

Functional Areas of the Cerebral Cortex

1. **Visual Area:**
   Sight
   Image recognition
   Image perception

2. **Association Area**
   Short-term memory
   Equilibrium
   Emotion

3. **Motor Function Area**
   Initiation of voluntary muscles

4. **Broca's Area**
   Muscles of speech

5. **Auditory Area**
   Hearing

6. **Emotional Area**
   Pain
   Hunger
   "Fight or flight" response

7. **Sensory Association Area**

8. **Olfactory Area**
   Smelling

9. **Sensory Area**
   Sensation from muscles and skin

10. **Somatosensory Association Area**
    Evaluation of weight, texture,
    temperature, etc. for object recognition

11. **Wernicke's Area**
    Written and spoken language comprehension

12. **Motor Function Area**
    Eye movement and orientation

13. **Higher Mental Functions**
    Concentration
    Planning
    Judgment
    Emotional expression
    Creativity
    Inhibition

Functional Areas of the Cerebellum

14. **Motor Functions**
    Coordination of movement
    Balance and equilibrium
    Posture

Reflective Notes

New learning and understanding need to find a secure place to take root in the brain's network. This task is more easily accomplished when new information is presented in manners that engage with the senses. As a facilitator or organizer, how can you create meaningful learning experiences for your participants? Remember as you answer that task/work should be thoughtful, purposeful, and have relevance to the work your participants are engaging.

1.
2.
3.
4.
5.
6.
7.

Additional items I want to remember as to brain compatibility and its integration with professional development training:

_____
_____
_____
_____
_____
_____
_____

Educators desire professional development structures that foster collaboration and are most satisfied when relevance to day-to-day work are clear!

CHAPTER 2

Structure & Preparedness

Since I started writing this book, I have been asked to conduct several professional development sessions. A few I turned down as to the time constraints involved with the publishing of the book; but others I felt would advance my research and/or my experience. One of the sessions I decided to facilitate was located in the northern part of the United States and consisted of more than eight hundred teachers. The session was offered via an eight-hour Web-based training. Before I move on, I must add that this was the school district's first Web-based training, so we were all a little worried as to the "what-ifs."

After working on the PowerPoint presentation and with my co-facilitator over the course of a month, the time finally arose as to the day before the training. The organizer contacted us wanting to conduct a sound check and walk-thru as to equipment and site transmittal (fifteen sites very engaged) connectivity. Upon arrival, my co-facilitator and I were asked to conduct a pre-session with the on-site facilitators as to our presentation. While I thought this meant a quick review as to content, their roles and responsibilities etc., the organizer actually meant a complete run-thru as to the delivery and review of slides, verbiage, and presentation. As the facilitators, we obliged and conducted a run-thru of the presentation. While conducting the run-thru, the chat box overflowed as to the facilitators' unpre-

paredness and inability to facilitate their small-group activities as previously discussed.

Long story short, the school district there was divided into two sections: one section whose facilitators were familiar with the information being discussed the next day as they were actively implementing the curriculum and concepts; and the other whose admin team told them to revert back to their prior manner of instructing if they had questions as to implementation or implication for the at-risk population served. Thus they did not have the skills/knowledge necessary to facilitate small-group activities/discussions. The result: panic, turmoil, and dismay, of course—a lengthy chat session.

At this point, the organizer, my co-facilitator, and I gathered to discuss the next courses of action, implementation strategies, and changes needed to warrant ease of facilitation. After a few hours of thinking outside the box, we decided to implement a few strategies, one of which was to craft a PowerPoint presentation for facilitators depicting their roles and responsibilities, but also outlining ours with special cues as to what they should implement and when. We also stressed that I would provide contextual cues and prompts during delivery as to timing and site-based activities. At this point, our overall objective was to lessen the impact of these facilitators on attendees while also ensuring the on-site facilitators had enough information, material, and knowledge to be impactful and able to successfully implement planned activities.

The results of this impromptu process actually enhanced our facilitation and implementation of the training as we were more cautious as to the learning objectives and ensured that we were stressing various components and connecting the dots as we matriculated through the content and activities. Learning goal: always be adaptable and OPEN!

The structure of the presenter, agenda, and framework all work in tandem to ensure optimal delivery and learning objectives are met in order for teacher professional development to be effective, memorable, and of high quality—all reflective of best practices and brain research.

The structure of an item attests to its ability to stand firm, to withstand damage and turmoil, and is indicative of strength and strong will. The structure of a professional development offering should be no different. In order for a training, conference, or workshop to be effective, the basis or support structure supporting it must also be effective. Components of structurally sound professional development offering reveals itself via the organizer's ability:

1. To understand the needs of the training;
2. To establish learning goals;
3. To document desired outcomes;
4. To forecast budgets;
5. To establish evaluation tools;
6. To ensure an inviting and inspiring room décor, well-thought-out and prepared meals and,
7. To be mindful of participants' expectations and experiences.

Further preparedness is centered on the presenters/facilitators preparedness, their understanding of the subject matter, audience, and his/her ability to articulate the subject matter clearly using varied mediums. Participants also hold accountability measures as they:

1. Present prepared for learning with any prior assignments mastered.
2. Prepared to share and document prior knowledge/past experiences.

3. Understand the objectives and content presented and how these relate to them.
4. Arrive eager to engage and incite robust and invigorating discussions and points of reference.

Lastly structure lies within environment as to:

1. Space (size, atmosphere, parking);
2. Meals;
3. Staffing needs;
4. Room (temperature, furniture);
5. Tools necessary to implement the training (flip charts, technology, learning resources, etc.); and
6. Learning goals and the manner in which organizers have communicated the intended and desired goals to the presenter/facilitator.

Organizers are especially vital in the planning and preparation of professional development sessions. It is the organizers' task to share the learning objective and to clearly articulate their goals and vision of the day. In fact, each professional development session offered should begin with the establishment of vision, goals, and objectives and then plan backwards (my hubby would say ... this is called backwards planning) as to goal achievement and placing a plan in action.

Optimal structural planning mandates that organizers decipher potential threats, perform tactical analysis, and limit the potentiality of negative experiences and disruptions during professional development trainings. (While these seem technical and unnecessary, note that it only takes one incident or person to derail a well-planned-out training.) Additional attention should be concerned with the experience of the attendees and presenters as well as mission accomplishment.

 As an organizer, a checklist of the following will help to ensure goal attainment, thus mission accomplishment:

- Establishment of pertinent learning goals
    o Should be limited to no more than four (two for half-day sessions);
    o Goals must be communicated to the presenter and attendees;
    o Agenda must be designed to facilitate goal attainment and optimized to facilitate engagement of the executive brain functioning (higher-level thinking) skills and participant engagement.

- Alignment to the manners in which adults learn
    o Survey or knowledge of the attendees as to their experience, education, and years in the field;
    o Opportunities for participants to exchange ideas and engage in discussions and problem-solving activities;
    o Integration of various learning medians in the delivery structure and the venue to support (hands-on/group activities, role plays, small group vs. large, etc.).

- State or lead organization standards
    o Knowledge as to priorities, initiatives, and best practices and the impact of these;
    o Budget adherence—staying on track and in focus;
    o State requirements—professional development topics one must include;
    o Agenda establishment detailing the flow of the day but also ensuring adherence to best practices as to implementation vs. organizational needs and structures.

To ensure optimal planning and preparedness, plan your professional development trainings with the following best practices:

1. What systems need to be in place to support participants as they engage in professional development opportunities?

2. What types of needs assessments will participants need to engage in to establish goals?

3. What types of research and studies will participants need to engage in to inform their instructional practices?

4. How will participants/organizers document, assess, and make their learning objectives and progress public?

5. How will participants/organizers set new goals as the need changes and old ones are met?

6. What types of resources will participants/organizers need to access in order to engage in a variety of professional learning experiences?

7. What steps have been taken to access participants' needs and to obtain their buy-in and support?

Also critical during the planning stages are needs assessments. Below is an example of one I have found to be beneficial:

Data Source:
- What is the data telling you?
- What sources of data should you triangulate?
- What levels of differentiated intervention does the data refer?
- How vast is the data in scope?

Participant Skills:
- What do participants need to know and be able to address?
- What additional content information should teachers possess?
- What supports do facilitators need to better provide strategy and foster skill attainment?

Organizational outcomes:
- What outcomes do you want for your organization/students/school?
- Are there gaps between the data and the desired outcomes? If so explain.
- Are there content gaps?
- What related interventions or supports are needed for total goal attainment?

Trajectory of professional development supports:
- What professional development is needed?
- What will the learning structures entail?
- What sequence of implementation makes the most senses? Content?
- Have I encouraged and offered opportunities for group interactions and peer-to-peer support and engagements?

> - What are the most effective manners to meet participants' needs?
> - How will you know if you are meeting your goals?
> - How is success evaluated?

> What steps will you take to revisit this plan throughout the year to inform practice, make revisions, and foster growth and accountability?

The main objective of the facilitator is to ensure the learning objective is mastered using a variety of methods and techniques designed to engage participants. Best practices reflect:

- Demonstration of clear and concise understanding of the learning objective and desired participant outcomes.

- Delivery method of the material – Web-based, hands-on experimental learning, discussion groups, and those activities or dialogue sessions designed to foster growth.

- Elimination of terminology that will be new to more than 90 percent of the group or a concerted manner in which to introduce terminology that fosters understanding and immediate association. (If the term cannot be immediately associated, it remains in short-term memory for a brief period of time and then is eliminated if association or transferability is not associated within thirty-six hours.)

- Presentation style referring to the delivery of information – This should be varied in terms of tone, voice inflictions, eye contact, the moving about the room vs. standing at a podium, the manner in which the presenter addresses the audience, and his/her demeanor and sincerity. Use stories to highlight learning objectives and facilitate understanding.

- Ability to assimilate with the audience while maintaining your position as the facilitator.

- Communication with participants – Using concise, simple, and easy-to-understand language that not only engages participants but also challenges growth (being aware of technical language, stats, and connotations).

Three years ago I hired a facilitator to present to a group of teachers. In the discovery conversations as to goals, mission, learning objectives, and so on, I asked the facilitator to discuss with me the manner in which she communicated with her participants. She began by stating, "What do you mean, 'communicate?'" I simply restated and emphasized "communicate." She responded, "When I ask a question, they should answer. After all, I am the presenter and I am here to share with them my expertise and knowledge."

While her answer was partially true, the implementation of her skills from the discovery phase to obtainment was unfilled and I decided to investigate another facilitator. This decision was easy for me, as while I am experienced and knowledgeable, I alone do not have all of the answers and cannot assume my audiences are empty vessels waiting to be filled solely with my knowledge alone.

Of course, this action conjured many issues as the presenter is one that had been used for years on end and I must add used exclusively ... so much so that she quit her job to present for my organization alone. Yet, I was not liable for her livelihood; I was liable for ensuring the teachers under my purview obtained the skill set, education, and resources needed to impact quality education and to ensure our students were making progress on a continuous basis. I must also add that a year and a half ago I saw this facilitator at a statewide meeting. She began by hugging and then thanking me as to my commitment to high training standards. She stated that she had been facilitating for so long she had lost sight of the needed interactions and reasons for discussion, questions, etc. To date, I have seen this person morph into a fantastic facilitator, one who is conscientious and aware of her audience and able to place the needs and learning styles of her attendees before her own.

A participant's role in professional development is more aligned with preparedness than structure as the majority have little to do with the organization and implementation of such; yet they should present prepared and eager to learn new skills. Participants should present with the following preparedness best practices:

- Arrive on time, with learning at the core of their interest and intent.

- Have materials in hand, having read supplies/materials prior.

- Actively ready to engage in discussions; open mind.

- An understanding of what the presentation is about; knowledge of the learning objectives and outcomes and potential takeaways.

- Knowledge as to agendas, breaks, and opportunities to take care of personal needs (childcare, telephone conversations, meals and snacks, center/school emergencies, etc.).

- An understanding of how the presented topics/content reflect their organizational/school structure and implementation procedures.

- The duration of this PD offering and its connection to additional learning practices, theories, webinars, and concepts.

When participants are prepared, the learning objectives are materialized in a fashion that breathes success, thus constituting a win-win situation for all. The session then becomes more engaging and insightful as to discussions/activities, which aid in the learning phase and ultimately goal acquisitions and transformations!

Ben was a teacher at a local school where I routinely facilitated professional development sessions. Ben would always appear eager to attend and would participate in discussions, yet during lectures and/or group time he seemed disinterested and frankly annoyed. The third time I had the pleasure of facilitating a session in which he attended I noticed the same behavior, so I decided to speak to him on the first break.

Ben commented that he completed his task as he participated in the first hour and would now relax and take care of his business, which involved playing and interactions with this BlackBerry. I remember commenting to him as to lack of participation and how this would negate peer-to-peer discussions as well as goal transmittal once he returned to his school. He commented, "It's okay. They will cover for me." Ben is an example of teachers who attend trainings and check the box—then check out.

My task was to re-engage Ben by making the content and learning objectives applicable to him. Yes, this is part of the facilitator's dance—the ability to engage, assimilate, re-engage, and employ tactics and activities to meet your audiences' needs and learning styles. In doing so, I not only reengaged Ben, but many others whose names I will never know.

The point remains that while we (as presenters) employ various topics, we will still meet the Bens of the world who present

> *as interested then morph into the been-there-done-that syndrome. Therefore the challenge becomes ensuring participants are and remain connected to the materials at hand.*

ENVIRONMENT

> *It was a dark and stormy night.... The breeze wafted gently across the white, silky sand....*

Immediately, readers/listeners begin to imagine the scene in their minds. As each descriptor is read, another element is visualized that adds content to the picture/scene creating mental images and intent, thus the creation of the setting.

Now, picture this setting:

> *Its 8 a.m. and the first participants are just arriving. As they enter the classroom, they noticed slogans and schedules about the room. Also displayed are names of teams and supporting material to accompany several activities. Displayed on the overhead are the words "Teach for Understanding." These words begin to create chatter and cause many to reflect immediately as noted during quick observations. The tables are grouped in semi-circles with one row encasing the other. As the facilitator began her opening, she asked for responses to the words on the overhead. She also incites discussions from peers and other participants as to the conversation and their teaching philosophy.*

Effective professional development offerings have been found to be sustainable, ongoing, site-based, and afford teachers the opportunity to collaborate on a number of different activities, practices, and concepts. Environmental preparedness constitutes a variety of elements from that of organizational knowledge, to that of personnel support to cleanliness, room setup, and IT prep. This is an area where no matter how good the presenter is, the environment can derail a structurally sound professional development offering.

Well-designed professional development settings are essential in promoting and supporting teachers' development of new content knowledge and effective instructional practice. In these types of settings, teachers engage in intellectually deep conversations and close inspections of curriculum, teaching, and student learning issues. Such settings are integral to the everyday life of successful schools.

While the ultimate goal of professional development is to improve student learning, the elements of the setting (place, time, participants, activity, and resources) require careful planning to support ongoing collaboration to achieve this goal. In settings designed for learning, the participants understand their responsibilities, the shared goal, and know they need to support one another in achieving the goal.

Settings designed for learning imply the involvement of a more knowledgeable and skilled person who can assist the learning of another through deliberate and supportive interactions (Rosemary, 2009).

In well-designed settings, participants collaborate in setting goals, engaging in meaningful activity, and assisting one another in achieving them. In well-designed settings, participants reflect on students and teachers learning through close analysis of evidence, which they use to improve teaching. Coaches and teachers work in iterative cycles of examining data, establishing goals, evaluating, reflecting, and revising. It is not easy to create settings in which progress is sustained and the hard work of the coaches and teachers is validated by increases in student learning.

Progress ebbs and flows as coaches and teachers enter new relationships and work together in unfamiliar ways and in unfamiliar roles. The development of professional learning settings requires thoughtful planning by teachers, coaches, administrators, and other school personnel, as well as mutual commitment from all to the learning enterprise. Additionally, professional development settings that support the development of reflective practice are structured to allow time for practitioners to engage in collaborative inquiry, which heightens opportunities for reflection and correlates to optimal delivery of content, thus optimal transformations as depicted by research and best practices.

When professional development is designed and implemented according to researched-based principles, it can positively affect teachers' knowledge and practice. This is likely when the setting is planned to support content-rich activity and ample opportunity for substantive conversation connecting theory and practice.

The professional learning setting should be organized so the content can be adapted to address various aspects of the instruction and student needs. For example, if a literacy coach led a demonstration, discussion, and lesson planning focused on Know, Want to Know, Learn (K-W-L) for a third-grade teacher, the demonstration would not necessarily reach all teachers participating in the sessions unless the coach took into consideration the grade levels represented in the teacher group and presented alternatives based on specific characteristics of the groups' students. In relation to the scenario described previously, the teachers' knowledge also needs to be considered. For example, what do the teachers know about text structure? What instructional strategies do they know (Rosemary, 2009).

Best practices to implement in terms of environmental preparedness include:

1. Room Cleanliness/Temperature/Décor.

2. Learning activities are able to be conducted both via small and large groups as articulated to presenter.

3. Opportunities to reflect are incorporated and are offered.

4. Agendas and goals are clearly stated and resources available to support.

5. Safe places are incorporated (areas within a space where participants are allowed to take a break, de-stress, or remove themselves from participation without questions—usually for five minutes or so).

    o Opportunities to reflect on the subject matter/to engage with other attendees.

    o Address calls or emergencies or handle personal situations.

6. Designated or communicated space for meals, breaks, etc.

7. IT or someone on hand to handle technology issues as they arise.

8. Offer support – information desk/table etc.

The professional learning settings described at the beginning helps to summarize the features of a setting designed for professional learning. The third-grade-level teacher group depicted earlier could be any subject or grade-level group of teachers who train together routinely as part of their school's professional learning community while their goals primarily relate on improving teaching competencies to improve student learning. A thoughtfully planned agenda focuses their work; the workspace is conductive to productivity as their resource needs are met and designed to facilitate both small- and large-group work. Their learning goals are clearly articulated and understood and environment fosters support for creativity, brainstorming, opportunity for growth, and insightful discussions.

Reflective Notes

Structure and preparedness alike are core to optimal implementation of professional development. What items will you integrate into your structure and why? What changes are you anticipating? Do you anticipate any negative chatter or effects?

1.
2.
3.
4.
5.
6.
7.

Additional notes or reflection items to ponder regarding structure and preparedness:

_____
_____
_____
_____
_____
_____
_____
_____
_____

In the twenty-first century, working environments are evolving into collaborative places where knowledge is disseminated by autonomous individuals organized into more lateral and less hierarchical structures.

CHAPTER 3

Delivery Methods

"While professional development might not be the most controversial topic in education, its importance must not be minimized," said Jim Hull, NSBA senior policy analyst. He said the new educational standards will require teaching techniques that are substantially different from practices that are in place today; and it will take time not just to teach those techniques but to give teachers a chance to implement them effectively.

Reports galore are revealing that workshop-based professional development is ineffective, yet more than "90 percent of teachers participate in workshop-style training sessions during a school year." This section of best practices will explore the myriad of options associated with professional development implementation. As you read this section, you will note reference to Howard Gardner's Multiple Intelligences and Malcolm Knowles's Theories on How Adults Learn. Additionally, reflection and notes are associated with Dr. Marcia Tate's Professional Learning Strategies That Engage the Brain. Essentially, I have conducted research and have complied the best practices as to manners in which to deliver quality training using innovative, factual, and brain compatible methods.

As a review of the references noted above please familiarize yourself with the following:

Howard Gardner: Multiple Intelligences

Many of us are familiar with three general categories in which people learn: visual learners, auditory learners, and kinesthetic learners. Beyond these three general categories, many theories of and approaches toward human potential have been developed. Among them is the theory of multiple intelligences, developed by Howard Gardner, Ph.D., Professor of Education at Harvard University. Gardner's early work in psychology and later in human cognition and human potential led to the development of the initial six intelligences. Today there are nine intelligences and the possibility of others may eventually expand the list. These intelligences (or competencies) relate to a person's unique aptitude set of capabilities and ways they might prefer to demonstrate intellectual abilities.

The theory of multiple intelligences also has strong implications for adult learning and development. Many adults find themselves in jobs that do not make optimal use of their most highly developed intelligences (for example, the highly bodily kinesthetic individual who is stuck in a linguistic or logical desk job when he or she would be much happier in a job where they could move around, such as a recreational leader, a forest ranger, or physical therapist). The theory of multiple intelligences gives adults a whole new way to look at their lives, examining potentials they left behind in their childhood (such as a love for art or drama) but now have the opportunity to develop through courses, hobbies, or other programs of self-development.

MALCOLM KNOWLES: THEORY OF ADULT LEARNING

To document differences between the ways adults and children learn, Malcolm Knowles (1980) popularized the concept of andragogy ("the art and science of helping adults learn"), contrasting it with pedagogy ("the art and science of teaching children"). He posited a set of assumptions about adult learners—namely, that the adult learner:

- Moves from dependency to increasing self-directedness as he/she matures and can direct his/her own learning;

- Draws on his/her accumulated reservoir of life experiences to aid learning;

- Is ready to learn when he/she assumes new social or life roles;

- Is problem centered and wants to apply new learning immediately; and

- Is motivated to learn by internal, rather than external, factors.

Inherent in these assumptions are implications for practice. Knowles (1984) suggests that for adult learners facilitators should:

- Set a cooperative climate for learning in the classroom;

- Assess the learner's specific needs and interests;

- Develop learning objectives based on the learner's needs, interests, and skill levels;

- Design sequential activities to achieve the objectives;

- Work collaboratively with the learner to select methods, materials, and resources for instruction; and

- Evaluate the quality of the learning experience and make adjustments, as needed, while assessing needs for further learning.

Dr. Marcia Tate : Professional Learning Strategies That Engage the Brain

Brain research is confirming what staff developers have always known—that learning must be linked to real-life experiences for the learner to retain and later apply what is being taught (Tate, 2012). Because adults experience difficulties in separating their background of experiences from who they are personally, it is recommended and even encouraged that adults engage in reflective learning which allows them to assess and reassess their personal assumptions while being open to the ideas of others. It is equally important to offer content in various formats thereby engaging both hemispheres of the brain. Thus crossing the left hemisphere with the right takes a concept from thought to realization thereby increasing the capacity for the concept to be placed into practice.

Below are a sampling of strategies Dr. Tate documents as integral to include when facilitating PD using brain-smart methodologies (engaging the brain fully).

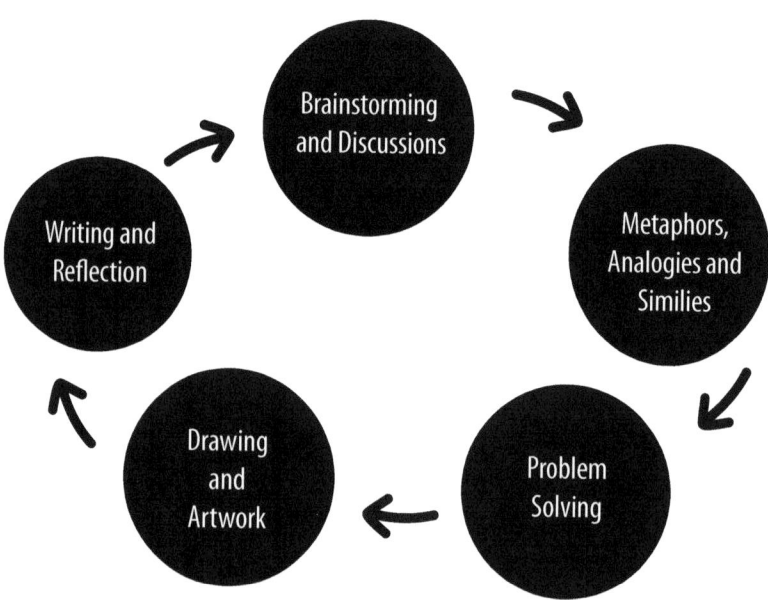

Brainstorming and Discussions. Questions posed during these activities will yield rich discovery as to key concepts facilitators want participants to learn and engage and the avenues for accomplishing such.

Sample question: What indicators will you receive when a participant has reached his/her goal? Is the goal continuous or a one-time feat/quest? Are additional support structures warranted? Learning objectives? Modifications?

Metaphors, Analogies, and Similes. One of the brain's primary jobs is to make meaning or to look for patterns and connections between what one already knows and newly inquired information. Thus when a new concept is being taught, it should be compared to one your participants already know and understand, thereby forming neural connections. Dr. Tate provides this example of metaphors, analogies, and similes: "By the time I finish teaching a workshop on the physiology of the brain, participants have stood and cupped their hands to resemble a three-pound brain, wiggled their fingers to stimulate the corpus callosum, raised their arms as metaphors for a neuron, tapped the palm of their hands to identify the cell body of neurons, and run their hands down their arms to recognize the axon of the neuron." Dr. Tate concluded by saying that once these items are performed, participants are asked to document their remembrance of the brain and its function, and revealed that most often participants are correct in their documentation. The connector here is the ability to associate metaphors, analogies, and similes with the manners in which adults learn and how these are integral to brain engagement and memory development.

Problem Solving. Professional learning opportunities designed at solving real-world problems are the most effective, thus transformative. This level of engagement involves both hemispheres of the brain and increases use of Bloom's Taxonomy. Problem solving takes a situation from a page or thought into actionable and scalable issues, which are large components of how adults learn. Facilitators engaging in implementation of this sort must ensure they fully understand the subject matter at hand as problem solving often conjures other frames of reference, which if ill prepared could result in attendees' summation of the presenter being in over his/her head or not prepared. Key points to include in the problem-solving delivery mode are:

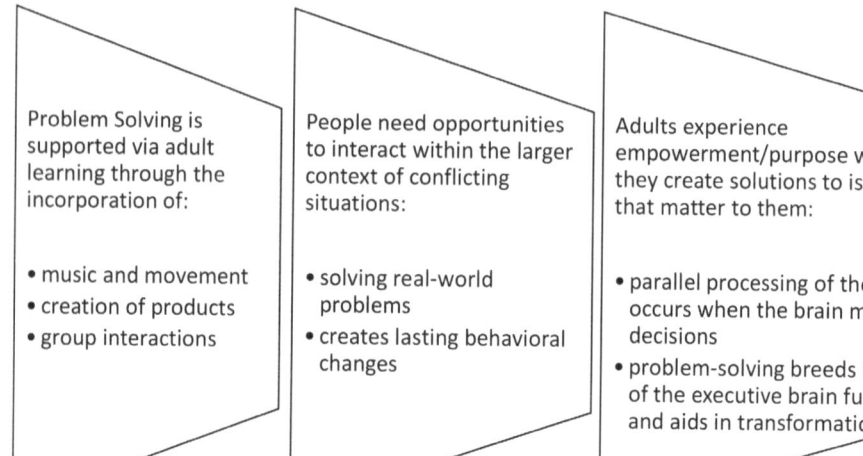

Drawing and Artwork. Many adults learn by spatial intelligence (one of Gardner's Multiple Intelligences); therefore workshop offerings that allow and support doodling, drawing, and encourage students' ability to decipher their understanding through pictorial representations are those considered brain-smart friendly. Dr. Tate stated she asked her "workshop participants to draw a human brain to remind them that procedural memory involves the use of the body, a smiley face to recall that positive thinking strengthens memory, and a face with a frown to symbolize the threats that extreme stress, anger, and fear can have on the body."

Writing and Reflection. Adult learning theory states that adults need guided opportunities to reflect on new knowledge and competencies. Journaling and note taking are the best methods for facilitating such reflection. During this process, Dr. Tate documents that acquisition of knowledge and skills are facilitated. Furthermore, she stated it is not the experience that creates learning; it is the reflection on that experience. Writing is another component that engages both hemispheres of the brain as the left hemisphere is key to that of language acquisition while the right hemisphere is engaged in the rationalization of emotionally difficult decisions and in the production of original ideas.

Speaker Series are the most common type of professional development offerings made available throughout the world. It is noted that more than half of the adults attending these series need the human connection to be held accountable and to be responsive. Yet speaker series are ones considered ineffective if they consist of lecture-only delivery methods and endless use of PowerPoint. To increase these offerings, speaker series should be conducted with the objectives and outcomes fully displayed. Also included should be a variety of hands-on learning opportunities, group work, and the sharing of concepts through discussions and roundtables. While I am not opposed to speaker series, I am opposed to the mundane nature of the old implementation practices of speaker series that only include one-way communication. Additionally, it is imperative that speakers serve more as facilitators, which is indicative of transformative learning and aids in optimal learning—best practices.

❖ For speakers/lecturers and/ or facilitators to fully engage their audience, the topics presented must be presented in a brain-smart manner, which includes:

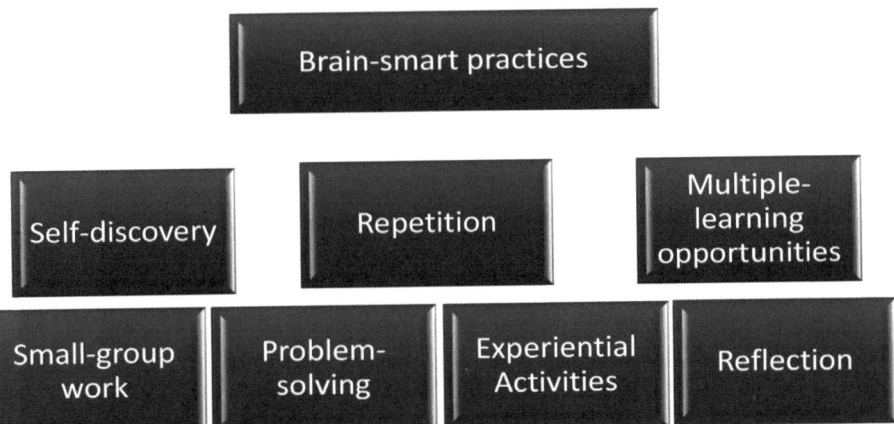

❖ Integrating educational theories, teaching strategies, and other andragogy tools in meaningful and useful ways to better address the needs of adults have proven for years to be successful in the professional development courses I have planned and coordinated. Gardner himself asserts that educators should not follow one specific theory or educational innovation when designing instruction, but instead employ customized goals and values appropriate to their teaching and the learner's needs.

Addressing the multiple intelligences and potential of adult learners can help facilitators personalize instruction and methods of evaluation, thus taking time to understand one's audience (background, educational levels, experiences in the field, prior instruction received, learning methodology, and if possible, the types of learners in the audience) is core to optimal skill attainment and thorough understanding of concepts/best practices.

> *Learning one's audience is one that sounds strange, but if performed correctly will take a professional development session from the mundane to the extraordinary. I remember a PD session I coordinated and facilitated my first year at the United Way of Metropolitan Nashville. While the topic is not important, the fact that I took a week to ask questions, research my audience, and to determine a plan of action that met 95 percent of my audience's educational and professional goals is important.*

> *So how was this possible? I took the time to meet with the twelve literacy coaches assigned to these ninety-four teachers. I also researched their educational levels and tailored my presentation to reflect the manners in which adults learn and the components of brain development. I also modified my terminology to ensure I was not speaking at my audience but to my audience (this is HUGE and could be considered offensive).*

> *Note that if you are going to use a wide variety of terminology, ensure you introduce these terms to your audience (no matter*

what level you feel they are on) as it's better to be safe in your presentation than to lose half midway as they are trying to decipher your words and use context cues to determine meaning. Side note: When presenters learn their audience, they become vested in the session and place themselves in positions to teach and share instead of just strictly being the knowledge holder and facilitator.

Instructional Coaching. Instructional coaching is grounded in current research and clinical knowledge on leadership and schools as "professional communities of practice." Recent research on professional development suggests that coaching is most effective when it includes components based in the school and embedded in the job and when it increases teachers' theoretical understandings of their work (Miller, 2010).

Supports for improved teaching and learning are also more effective when they are tailored to needs identified by teachers and when their approach to learning is collaborative and inquiry-based (Darling-Hammond and McLaughlin, 2012). Coaching provides such supports through an array of activities designed to build collective leadership and continuously improve teachers' instructional capacity. These activities, ideally, coalesce in ways that create internal accountability due to the embedded nature of the work and people engaged in it (Barr, Simmons, and Zarrow, 2003). A well-designed and supported coaching program weds core elements of effective professional development with the essential goals of professional learning communities in ways that advance both facility and systemic improvement.

In 2011 I had the opportunity to work with a wonderful group of literacy coaches as they revamped the coaching model currently in place. During the process, I became consumed with the concept of intentional coaching and the needs/process of not only the model but also the intent of such and the actual methodologies of intentional coaching. As the model was reworked, it was apparent many of the coaches were just "doing the work" per se, as this is what was expected. Yet when they were informed as to best practices, behavioral changes were warranted and the zest for a better practice welcomed. The difference I uncovered was that of intentional coaching, proper documentation, and overall accountability. To date, the practice of intentional coaching remains effective and practiced routinely.

Teachers are open to this level of professional development and coaches are able to instruct based on need and progress—not merely subject matter and availability.

❖ Intentional coaching and instructional coaches are on-site change agents who use professional development and differentiated coaching to increase teacher effectiveness by teaching educators how to successfully implement effective, research-based teaching techniques and practices. Like differentiated instruction, differentiated coaching means tailoring coaching instruction to meet the individual needs of teachers. Instructional coaches apply a variety of professional development methods that encourage high-quality implementation of interventions, leading to sustainability of the newly acquired skills. Instructional coaches use guided reflective practices and a partnership approach to accelerate each teacher's professional learning.

As a "change agent" the instructional coach must:

- Unfreeze current behavior: Create disequilibrium with the current state as an impetus to explore change;

- Cognitively restructure: Help teachers build new skills, strategies, methods, and behaviors using coaching strategies and professional development;

- Refreeze: Provide opportunities for teachers to practice the new skills until they are comfortable; and

- Create a culture of trust: A psychological safety net is developed so teachers feel comfortable failing and retrying (University of Oklahoma, 2011).

An intentional, meaningful, consistent, and reflective coaching process is an effective way for coaches to support teachers as they implement and sustain new instructional practices. For high-quality, effective coaching to occur, specific coaching skills and protocol must be learned and practiced continually with master coaches in the field of education. For sustained change to occur in the classroom, coaches need an opportunity to network with one another and learn from experts.

Coaching protocols as recommended by the University of Oklahoma are:

- Instructional coaches follow a routine protocol when working with teachers, observation, pre-conference, demonstration, and reflection/post-conference. This continuous cycle affords the teacher time to observe demonstrations and practice the new skills. In addition, the coach and teacher engage in reflective discussions and plan action steps for growth and change. It is a partnership based on trust.

- An instructional coach must be an expert in building relationships, even with those teachers who resist change. Providing continuous assistance until the skill has been learned, practiced, and sustained is essential. A coach's interaction with a teacher occurs for short periods of time. Such interaction provides help and assistance based on information gleaned through assessing and observation where teacher behavior is changed.

- Coaching should be regarded as a process that empowers teachers with reflective problem-solving skills. Fullan (1991) notes that we over-assume the capacity of teachers to move actively into implementation without a substantial amount of help and assistance. The approach to teacher development should be long-term and continuing over time in order to respond to teachers' needs as they are changing from novices to experts. An instructional coach bridges the gap, thus increasing teacher effectiveness and student outcomes.

Typical professional development models include more than one component and work in tandem to produce optimal outcomes for teachers and children. The model below is based on research conducted over an eight-year period at the University of Oklahoma. It includes:

- Appropriate classroom environment
- Research-based curriculum
- Content knowledge (consistent, ongoing professional development opportunities)
- Progress monitoring (leads to differentiated instruction)
- Instructional coaching

Coaching is the key that provides rigor and accountability to the model. Teachers with whom I work cite the following as strong preferences when designing a coaching program.

1. My coach knows what it's like to teach; to work with students, parents, and administrators.

2. My coach is considered an expert in the field.

3. Coaching sessions provide them with specific and actionable steps they can try in their classrooms immediately.

4. My coach consistently provides feedback, both orally and written.

5. My coach is understanding, patient, and supportive; not condescending.

6. My coach demonstrates a topic using various methods or a period of time.

7. My coach provides praise, accolades, and acknowledges my efforts.

❖ Effective coaching encourages collaborative, reflective practice. Coaching shifts professional learning from direct instruction outside the context of practice (such as workshops and conferences) to more varied opportunities to improve discipline-specific practice. Most studies show that coaching leads to improvements in instructional capacity. For instance, teachers apply their learning more deeply, frequently, and consistently than teachers working alone, thus improve their capacity to reflect. They apply their learning not only to their work with students but also to their work with each other.

❖ Effective embedded professional learning promotes positive cultural change. The impact of coaching often goes beyond improving content instruction. The conditions, behaviors, and practices required by an effective coaching program can affect the culture of a school or system, thus embedding instructional change within broader efforts to improve school-based culture and conditions (Neufeld and Roper, 2003).

Well-designed coaching models reflect three key components:

1. Structural conditions that support effective coaching, which include but are not necessarily limited to:

    • Clearly articulated school/curriculum initiatives and goals directly linked to expected coaching outcomes;

    • A content focus (such as literacy/numeracy);

    • Structural guidelines (coaching in groups or in individual settings);

- Systematic measurement of work and impact (data and evidence documentation);

- Generally accepted set of principles for adult learning, including collaborative, ongoing, job-embedded work that is actively constructed and refined by participants;

- Dedicated time for teacher groups to meet, learn together, analyze their work, observe each other, collect evidence of their work and its impact, and refine their practice and document;

- Established negotiable and non-negotiable congruent with center/school-based policies and procedures or funding guidelines.

2. A guided, content-based focus on adult learning in a school-based professional learning environment that enables coaches to:

   - Focus on data and evidence-informed learning;

   - Promote adult learning in a way that models classroom practice;

   - Construct and apply knowledge and skills in the classrooms of participating teachers;

   - Develop school and teacher learning plans that focus on content and leadership;

   - Make connections and ensure alignment within the larger system (philosophy, goals, mission);

   - Continuously measure, document, reflect upon, and adjust professional learning opportunities.

3. Instructional leadership by coaches who typically

- Observe instruction and provide feedback to teachers;

- Construct opportunities for groups of teachers to observe each other;

- Structure time for teachers to discuss their learning from classroom observations, modeled lessons, etc.;

- Model particular instructional strategies for individuals or groups of teachers;

- Employ multiple strategies to gather and analyze student evidence with teachers;

- Facilitate teacher meetings during professional development time, common planning time, coordinated before/after-school time, weekend work sessions;

- Support teachers in groups and, if necessary, individual settings;

- Engage in their own learning with other coaches and content specialists to improve their work.

Coaches must be knowledgeable not only in their content area but also in the areas of educational reform theories and goals, state, national, and local goals and initiatives, achievement standards, and adult learning. Meeting such a range of goals requires that coaches possess strong communication and interpersonal skills, consistently follow through with support for teachers, and demonstrate a willingness to listen and learn (Neufeld and Roper, 2003). The degree to which coaches possess these skills impacts the success of standards-based instruction in the classroom and the quality of links to district supports and broader school reform efforts.

Emerging evidence shows that teachers' success at changing practice mirrors the work of their coaches (Neufeld and Roper, 2003).

Professional Learning Communities (PLC) enhance the capacity of education practitioners and stakeholders to engage in collaborative work aimed at improving instructional programs and practices and increasing student learning across educational environments (schools, child development centers, districts, community agencies, etc.). Research demonstrates that the development of a strong professional community among educators is a key ingredient in improving schools (Langer, 2000).

PLCs afford teachers the ability to be innovative in their discussions and to share candidly as to best practices and challenges, all while documenting the process and recommendations. PLCs work best when embraced by administration and held as key in terms of attendance, allowing time for group work, documentation, and in observing. PLCs vary in their existence and makeup from one-on-one groups to small groups of three or four, to larger workgroups of five to seven.

To ensure candor, subscribe to best practices, and promote teamwork, it is recommended that these groups be limited to no more than six members (enough to pair equally if needed). The other variable is to ensue your PLCs are diverse in terms of demographics, ethnicity, location, and experiences (two years of teaching as opposed to that of ten). Remember, the goal is to promote reflection and engagement; therefore, the more diverse the group and experiences are, the more diverse and profound the results of the groups will be.

> *PLCs was not a strategy I was very familiar with, but one I researched two years ago as teachers inquired as to additional manners in which to seek knowledge and to collaborate with their colleagues. The result of a year of research is a robust learning community designed with a core emphasis on teachers' selected and specific topics presented in an interactive and brain-smart manner. Each quarterly training offered in this format involved a forty-five-minute facilitation or inquiry-based session followed by group work and/or problem-based learning that fully engaged the brain and allowed for personal reflection, insightful discussions, and incorporated hands-on learning opportunities. The end result was teachers who wanted to stay longer than their PD hours allowed and those whose experiences conjured additional questions as to the exposure. This is where each PD session should end—engaging so attendees are wanting to further explore the topics discussed and those who cannot wait to employ the strategies or concepts into their classrooms the following day.*

❖ Effective professional development to improve classroom teaching also concentrates on high learning standards and on evidence of students' learning.
It mirrors the kinds of teaching and learning expected in classrooms. It is driven fundamentally by the needs and interests of participants themselves, enabling adult learners to expand on content knowledge and practice that is directly connected with the work of their students in the classroom (Elmore, 2002).

❖ Understanding what motivates adults to grow and learn enhances professional development and helps the school or district become a community of learners (Zepeda, 1999). The PLC approach is grounded in adult learning theory and references several characteristics important to adult learners. For example, as autonomous and self-directed adults, professional educators need to be involved in the planning and evaluation of their instruction, as they often reject prescriptions by others for their learning. Adults have accumulated a foundation of experiences, knowledge, skills, interests, and competence. They are most interested in learning subjects that have immediate relevance to their jobs or personal lives. Like learners of all ages, adults need to see the results of their efforts and to get feedback about progress toward their goals (Zemke and Zemke, 1995).

❖ The effects of PLCs are optimized when they exist not in isolation but as part of overlapping, interconnected communities of practice (Resnick and Hall, 2001). Members of such "overlapping" communities are both formally and informally bound together by what they do, by what they have learned through their mutual engagement in the work, and through the work they have produced.

❖ Overlapping PLCs are unified by common goals but focus their work on affecting change from a variety of vantage points within the system. In this way, knowledge is created, shared, organized, revised, and passed on within and among these communities. As a result, schools are better positioned to construct organizational expertise and to develop strategies that ensure their individual work is connected to the larger educational goals.

Tools needed to ensure effective PLCs are:

- Connecting learning communities
    o Engage community organizations and other educational partners in a variety of activities to increase their overall capacity to support and monitor the implementation efforts.

- Technical assistance
    o Provides support as needed from administrators and coaches and/or encourages interactions with other PLCs.

    o Confers with local universities as to best practices, test measurements, understanding and defining rubrics.

    o Participates in larger PLCs and groups leading and advancing the work.

- Using tools to inform the work.
    o Rubrics describing key indicators and levels of enactment (e.g., beginning, emerging, sustaining, etc.) to identify/assess/analyze progress.

    o Frameworks for content and group process.

    o Video packages, which include guides for facilitators, on topics such as peer observation, looking at student work, and leadership development

    o Web-based resources portals to local and national efforts by researchers and practitioners to implement and inform best practices and concept implementation.

Book Studies/Lending Libraries is a learning experience that gives educators an opportunity for professional networking, sharing, and reflection through an in-depth examination of ideas, concepts, research, and strategies presented within a professional resource. When professional book club experiences are tied to the real work of teachers and to authentic issues they are grappling with in their classrooms, teachers have a deeper understanding of their impact on classroom practices and student learning. Book studies and lending libraries are fairly new to the professional development era, yet the benefits of those are directly linked to student achievement and goal acquisition.

Book studies were first discovered in biblical communities, as it was known as Bible study. Soon afterwards book studies and lending libraries came into play with romance novels. To date, book clubs are commonplace across various mediums and disciplines. In the educational sector, teachers alike share a variety of resources including books, documents, short stories, best practices, journals and peer-reviewed articles all with the same goal of education and in reviewing best practices with the hopes of increasing student performance and teacher accountability.

Lending libraries can take many forms including roaming, being singular in focus (items contained) or varied housing kits, theme boxes, databases, and catalogs, and can range from a sophisticated system to an old card catalogue system dating back ten to fifteen years. Taking each system into account, the real goal and purpose is to equip educators with additional tools and resources to stimulate classroom learning via the integration of new concepts and tools through high quality and accessible resources.

Personally, I have been integral in the design and development of four professional leaning library systems for early education teachers. Each one was designed a little differently based on audience, but the common thread was a wide array of material and resources available to teachers and the environment associated with both.

Best practice – I encouraged use of the library during PD training times and before/after work hours. I also incorporated incentives, snacks, and coffee/tea to mimic an inviting yet warm setting. Also included were notepads, computers, and other technological devises and manipulatives such as die-cut machines and laminators so teachers could use their planning time to research, prepare, and discuss with colleagues in a supported and nurturing environment. Through lending libraries and book clubs, learning becomes continuous and emphasizes self-directed learning, thus eliminating intimidation and fear of publicly speaking (workshops/trainings) or questioning.

"Book Club" Meetings. In this process, participants read selected relevant material and meet to discuss the topic on a regularly scheduled basis. Material can be books, articles, or even multimedia. Material should be chosen and endorsed by administrators. Organize an initial thirty-minute to one-hour session during a faculty meeting or other time regularly available to school leaders and teachers in the selected subject area. Four weeks in advance of the meeting send invitations to the participants explaining the purpose of the book club and assigning the assignments to group. During the meeting, you or the director can facilitate discussions. Conclude by inviting a staff member to facilitate the next discussion and assigning the next reading. You might request anonymous feedback on what teachers especially liked, did not like, and suggestions for improvement.

Ms. Irish Story:

Teaching is a passion of mine and has been for the past ten years. It wasn't until recently though, that I really began to enjoy the process of teaching. What happened? I obtained a new perspective and insight. You might say, I was inspired through the lens of a trainer. The training occurred at the United Way of Metropolitan Nashville. As the training ended, the facilitator challenged each of us to explore our goals and choices and to strive to instill the love of learning in our students through play. As I listened to her speak, I wondered how I would master this challenge. Then she invited each of us to join her in the newly designed professional lending library. The library presents with collection of teacher resource material (books, technological devices, videos, telescopes, camcorders, CDs, puzzles and other tools) to expand classroom practices and ensure teachers like myself are provided with insights as to why early education is important. It provided for me the rationale behind literacy and the various elements of literacy that I was not aware. Additionally, it provided for me self-confidence, which made me a better-more effective teacher who was now conscious of her choices, options and impact.

Within a few months' time, I checked out over 50 books and other material; finding each more helpful than the other. My classroom's structure has transformed into a child centered and focused environment where I am able to reach students on their individual levels and provide for them examples to ensure skill attainment. I'm proficient now and my students and colleagues are the benefactors. Many thanks to the creators of the library for embedding so many elements into my life and career.

Reflective Notes

When reviewing your professional development offerings, are your offerings aligned with those of Dr. Tate, Malcolm Knowles, or Howard Gardner? Are you meeting the learning style and needs of your teachers? Reflect on your current practices and the manner in which you can elevate these to the next level via the aforementioned chapter.

1.
2.
3.
4.
5.
6.
7.

Additional items I want to remember referencing delivery modes are:

_____
_____
_____
_____
_____
_____
_____
_____

Educators need empowerment. When professional development is personal and relevant, engagement and outcomes improve.

CHAPTER 4

Motivate & Inspire

When you wake up in the morning, what is the passion that fuels you to start your day? Are you living this in your work? If others asked you what drives you to achieve, would the answer be obvious? The numerous triggers that motivate people to achieve are unique for everyone.

> *Throughout my career I have had the pleasure of reinventing myself as my family relocated in support of my husband's assignments with the United States Army. During these transitions our kids and I often wondered...what's next? Where do we go from here and why? For Kent, my husband, his choices and path were clear. It was dictated by his unit losing and gaining and sandwiched somewhere within what I came to understand as the standard operating procedures (SOP). For us the pathway was cloudy; we had no SOP or direction and our fate was left to us.*
>
> *Of course there were kids for the boys to play with and school. But besides that, we were in charge of deciding how to assimilate to our new environments, how to climb whatever challenges were placed in front of us, and what tools we were going to use to handle these. Since the boys were young and Kent was absorbed with the transition, many of our family's elements/decisions were left to me. Motivation, you say; that's motivation, knowing your family's health and well-being are essentially in your hands and riding on your decisions/actions to keep them afloat.*

Motivation is not just centered on one's family health but also the individual's goals and well-being as well. As I traveled, continued my education, and discussed with other educators, I knew my motivation was one of equipping and transitioning with ease to lessen the impact on Kent and the boys and to provide them with peace of mind and security.

As educators, we too need peace of mind. We need growth opportunities both personally and professionally and to understand that our needs are important and warrant a discussion or an action plan. As I write this, I am reminded of a teacher within the Read to Succeed Program whom I will call Sherri. Sherri approached me to inquire as to manners in which she needed to take to become a better teacher. She stated, "I have been teaching now for fifteen years and I feel good as to what I do, but I am not sure of my effectiveness and drive anymore." She further stated, "I need to be better, for my students and for myself." Sherri's statement was the epitome of motivation; her drive for improvement was clear, as was her rationale. Yet in professional development sessions, the Sherri's of the world are often overlooked as the PD day is designed to meet the needs of the masses; instead of tailored to the audience and more specifically learners and their various degrees of learning styles.

When I use the term "motivation" within the scope of the Seven Best Practices, I am referencing the manner in which PD sessions are delivered. Are we motivating, inspiring, and challenging teachers to an action after the training; or are we just performing mundane trainings for the sake of performing the trainings; in hopes that someone will pick up a concept and implement or better yet, ask questions as to next steps?

Motivation and inspiration are key elements in the change paradigm, when transformative changes are embraced, they are essential to the learning process. It is generally proposed that adult learners come voluntarily into learning situations, and because of this, they will be motivated.

Yet this is not always the case; particularly in instances of compulsory attendance where seven out of ten attendees are depicted as mandatory.

Internal motivation comes from the drive within the individual to gain knowledge or a skill. Internal motivation may be influenced by external factors. External factors are those that place pressures on us but may not necessarily be converted into internal or psychological pressure. Better pay, promotions, or a better position are all indicators of external factors.

To incorporate motivation and inspiration into your professional development sessions, consider these simple yet profound courses of action that have proven to be effective in more than one hundred sessions conducted:

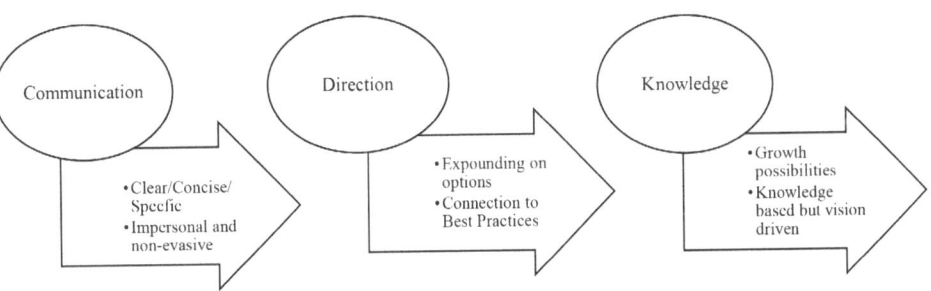

In addition to motivating and inspiring teachers, I also included vision board settings as a component of the regular PD trainings I offered. This is necessary if teachers are truly committed to the education field and want a trajectory of success and a solid education foundation on which to motivate. Simply speaking, if teachers want to move from being a pre-K teacher to an elementary school teacher, then to an administrator's role and so forth, providing teachers with the educational and baseline knowledge of the possibilities are equally important to the process.

Additionally, if teachers are teaching within non-traditional settings are a looking to achieve other positions within that framework, they must understand the goals, mission, and elements of the agency/organization to better situate themselves as credible candidates and to continuously demonstrate mastery of success. Vision boards, motivational techniques, and inspiration all serve as foundational tools to support this trajectory.

I must note that this is not a simple process or element; vision board and other inspirational elements should be visited often to ensure understanding and goal acquisition. In keeping with these views, Sciarra and Dorsey (2003) noted that motivation builds self-confidence and a sense of intrinsic job satisfaction and is essential to operational success.

Quarterly, administrators/directors can send staff an email as to goal acquisition and thoughts of inspiration and motivation. This simple task takes planning on your part but will yield great results as your staff will connect you to their professional development goals and achievements. And by reason they fail to progress, a director's motivating words and actions will eventually aid in teacher accountability, thus success. (I planned months in advance so that all I needed to do was implement on the due date. I just located the file and then pressed the send button—several times.)

Allow staff to include their vision and individual professional plans as a component to their professional learning communities. Remember the phrase "success breathes success"—motivation comes in many forms, across many languages, people, and circumstances. One's motivation may be discovered in the most unlikely places. Your embracement of these discussions will only advance the work, thus the education field, and will result in happier employees whose productivity will enhance as they feel valued and supported. Remember, professional development is multifaceted and begins with administrators setting the tone!

Consider the following as a part of a motivational strategy when establishing professional development plans and overall when working with your personnel:

1. Do you personally thank staff for a job well done? Are they aware you care about their personal growth and achievements?

2. Is performance and development feedback timely and specific?

3. Do you make time to meet with—and listen to—staff on a regular basis?

4. Is your workplace open, trusting, and fun?

5. Do you share information about your organization with staff on a regular basis? Do they understand how they impact the mission of the center/school?

6. Do you involve staff in decisions, especially those that will affect them personally and impede upon their professional growth attainment?

7. Do you give teachers the chance to succeed, to establish a trajectory of success or a vision as to their future?

As director of Fayetteville Technical Early Education Center, I awarded Monday Morning Smiles each Monday to my team. On Mondays I circulated a weekly newsletter as to center-wide information and updates. A component of this was a section entitled "Monday Morning Smiles." This section recognized teachers' hard work, but also accomplishments. For example, if someone completed a training session, went above the call of duty, assisted a co-worker, or simply found an article related to a certain topic and shared it with others, I recognized these actions with a sixteen-ounce bottle of their favorite beverage (usually soft drinks, juices, or water) and simply adhered a smiley face sticker on the bottle and placed them in the teachers' lounge with a personal note.

Everyone wanted to be recognized so the motivation was set ... again a simple method of recognizing advancement and hard work, but one that yield fruits and cooperation and planted seeds of success. Additional thank-you's and support manifested itself in the forms of teaching team lunches or allowing teachers to leave or arrive early/late as a method of appreciation. During these times, I would serve as their substitute or a classroom support structure.

The trainer's job is to motivate adults to learn. You can awaken their motivation to learn; you cannot force it. Adults learn effectively when they want:

- To develop a new skill

- To acquire new information

- To fulfill inner desires

- To improve professional competence

Adults learn best when what they are taught seems useful. Most attend training because they want to be there and because they've chosen to learn something new. However, they need to buy into the value of training. Trainers need to uncover issues that will motivate adults to participate.

One common tool within educational environments is the professional development plan which allows educators and administrators the ability to chart aspirations and growth via demonstration of skill attainment, documentation of success, and ultimately goal achievement. This plan should not be cumbersome for educators but should serve as a natural growth plan and directional guide. Because administrators/directors share in the setting of goals and aspirations, they are equally responsible to ensure goals are realized and most importantly hold their educator accountable.

Reflective Notes

Your role in motivating and inspiring your team is vast and for many will be instrumental in the realization of their goals. Reflect on the processes you will employ to ensure your team is successful, establishing realistic goals and objectives, and is remaining motivating/inspired when juggling task after task.

1.
2.
3.
4.
5.
6.
7.

Additional notes from the chapter:
_____
_____
_____
_____
_____
_____
_____
_____
_____

Professional development is most effective when teachers walk away with tools, lessons, and collaborators they can implement right away.

CHAPTER 5

Challenge and Engage

When done well, professional development challenges teachers with innovative possibilities, increases skills, and fosters ongoing conversation and collaboration to offer a challenge as a part of professional development that many people miss or feel should be self-imposed. To challenge someone is to provide for them a reason as to why they should act in a certain manner or change the manner in which they currently practice, think, employ, etc. To engage, on the other hand, reminds me of the old saying: "If you give a man a fish he eats for a day; however, if you teach him to fish he has the propensity to eat each and every day thereafter, as he now possess the skills to do so."

To engage adults in the learning process is to provide them with skills to make learning transformative. As stated earlier, transformational learning is the process of taking an idea, practice, or concept from stated words or mere acts to practice. This also involves the transferring of data from short-term memory to long-term memory.

Relating to best practices, challenging one after he/she has participated in professional development sessions increases the opportunity that they will engage and explore the materials learned, resulting in the transmittal of best practices, dialogue, and hopefully documentation as to the discoveries and advances in the field as well as teachable moments.

When participants are engaged they are able to demonstrate transmittal of the concepts taught and are thus more likely to transfer this knowledge into active learning and practice. It is my opinion that engagement and challenges work in tandem as to goal attainment and transformative learning. Best practices associated with the challenging and engaging elements are discussed below:

- To present a call to action as to the implementation of new knowledge to impede upon classroom practices and promote growth

- To foster the continuous quest for knowledge and learning as to quality of instruction and accountability

- To establish trust and garner interest

- The need to feel trusted, secure, and interested in the agenda is paramount. For example, students on the first day of class are preoccupied with assessing whether the teacher is going to be "nice" or "mean" and (secondarily) whether the class is going to be "fun." Similarly as adults, we seek to feel comfortable with our colleagues and to identify ways our goals might be met through participation in any given professional activity. In our efforts to fit well with others and to scope out the agenda, first meetings and first class days are occasions on which people tend to be on their best behaviors as they "get a feel" for the people and the agenda.

- Fostering ambitiousness helps clarify which rules, rewards, and resources are likely to be stable features of the learning and professional environment. Possibilities take on greater focus as teachers experience an analogous process in the school professional community. For example, they may commit to participate ambitiously in particular professional development activities to improve their instructional practices, or lean toward ambivalence, abstention, or resistance.

- Engage through play is designed as "any activity that engages the imagination." Imaginative engagement and play are synonymous and play is what allows us to dream up novel approaches, fresh plans, and creative solutions to unsolved problems. So make PD fun and actionable by having teachers work together to create things they can actually take back to use in their classrooms and share (make-n-takes).

- Allow teachers to develop useable lessons, ideas, and materials based on what they're learning so they can apply them to the specific curricula or topics they're teaching. Ask educators to bring their stories about students, successes, and concepts they're currently teaching and insert new technology and approaches where appropriate. Professional development is most effective when teachers walk away with tools, lessons, and collaborators they can use right away. (Engagement through play is as stated and outlined here supports Dr. Tate's brain-smart strategies discussed in the proceeding chapters).

- Encourage risk-taking: Once educators are connected and practicing their skills they will be much more likely to take chances; however, this takes time and confidence. Remember, meaningful PD must be continuous, on-demand, and social. Imagine being able to invite a trusted colleague into your classroom to watch your instruction, or better yet, to watch them teach to your students. Well, that is the idea behind embedded professional development and it helps to accelerate this process.

Joe Dixon (2015) documents the following engagement opportunities for educators as they undertake learning in a professional setting:

Start with the End in Mind. Professional development for the sake of professional development does little but waste the time and energy of teachers. Instead, encourage instructional leaders to define the goals for their unique learning community (e.g., provide quality reading instruction to improve student achievement or create a SOLE [self-organized learning environment].

Simultaneously, survey teachers to discover what each already knows and would like to accomplish. Once armed with this knowledge, it will be easier to plan embedded PD experiences that help your team achieve their goals. Having a clear understanding of the desired outcome is liberating and allows for true differentiation of instruction for each teacher.

Connect and Share. When conducting PD, the more intense the connection, the more effective the individual will be. In Edward Hallowell's book, Shine: Using Brain Science to get the Best from Your People, he writes about the importance of "Selection, Connection, Play, and one's ability to Grapple and Grow." Dr. Hallowell defines connection as "the bond an individual feels with another person, group, task, idea … or anything else that stirs feelings of attachment, inspiration, or a willingness to make sacrifices for the sake of the connection." As educators we intuitively understand the importance of connection and desire it in our interactions with our students and our peers.

Therefore, we must create the opportunity for connection and personalization in the professional development experiences we create. Build opportunities for educators to connect with each other and the topics being addressed. If teachers connect to the experience, they will continue to collaborate beyond the experience.

For Goodness' Sake, Have a Good Time. Again, let's turn to Dr. Hallowell, who defines play as "any activity that engages the imagination." Dr. Hallowell goes on to explain that imaginative engagement and play are synonymous and that play is what allows us to dream up novel approaches, fresh plans, and creative solutions to unsolved problems.

Therefore, professional development should be fun and actionable by incorporating group activities and demonstration of skills to create experiences they can immediately implement into their classrooms. This is a venue for teachers to develop useable lessons, create the professional development circles of support, generate ideas and materials based on what they're learning, and inquire as to the specifics for curricula or thematic integration.

Build a Culture of Risk-taking. Once educators are connected and practicing their skills they will be much more likely to take chances; however, this takes time and confidence. Remember, meaningful professional development must be continuous, on-demand, and social. Imagine being able to invite a trusted colleague into your classroom to watch your instruction, or better yet, to watch them teach to your students. This is the foundation of embedded professional development and it helps to accelerate the integration and learning process.

Teachers, and all people for that matter, are more likely to experiment when they are supported and receive immediate feedback from people they trust. Embedded PD takes many forms, in person/classroom both physically and virtually, as well as synchronous and asynchronous dialogue around recorded lessons, coaching sessions, and content introduced and skills attained. Embedded professional development is center to the professional development practices with the Read to Succeed structure and one that has moved our program from mundane to extraordinary. You can do this too; simply start small and you will be amazed how quickly your network will grow.

Build in Follow-up. Just as students require repeated review and testing to ensure key concepts have been grasped, professional development can't be a one-time happening that's then set aside until it's time for the next in-service.

Teachers should have the ability to go back and revisit PD tools and information, as well as ask clarifying questions once they've had the opportunity to use the recommended new skills or tools in the classroom. Providing deliberate follow-up reinforces new materials and also shows which developmental activities are yielding the most real-world value and results over time.

These key ideas open the door to a professional development program that empowers teachers and has lasting impact. Not only can professional development practices create an engaging, valuable, and a reinvigorating experience that educators look forward too, it can also be an effective tool for transforming the culture and performance of a school/early education center and a district.

Lastly, I would be remiss if I didn't add engagement via questioning as a best practice when implementing and connecting professional development. Questioning is definitely one of my favorite topics when it comes to teaching and learning. There is no question that in classrooms we emphasize answers much more than we do questions. And the questions we hear are more frequently teacher questions. Provocative questions tap into our natural inquisitiveness. Relevant questions spark the brain's search for personal connection and meaning. And by the way, forming answers isn't the only way for participants to engage in complex thinking ... forming questions can be equally challenging and revealing.

Only 32 percent of the educators in EdWeek's recent study, "Engagement Landscape," reported that they are "good at engaging and motivating [their] students" and only 14 percent "strongly agree that their in-service training provided such preparation." Thus teaches are oftentimes misusing one of the basic strategies for successful content attainment—questioning.

When educators are questioned during professional development sessions, not only are they introduced to new concepts/tips/techniques, but they are also prodded as to the usage and implementation of such as to how these practices should and might impact their classrooms, habits, and students. Furthermore, when used correctly, questioning engages ideas and concepts that may have been forgotten, reengages the uses of Bloom's Taxonomy, encourages participant collaboration, and clarifies implementation strategies/use and the extent of such.

Note that I am including a sample of Bloom's Taxonomy. Remember, at the center of the taxonomy is the connection to the brain and the manner in which we imply meaning, reason, and make sense of relayed information.

	Useful Verbs	Question Starters	Activities
Knowledge	Arrange Collect Define Describe Examine Label	What happened after…? Find the meaning of….? Can you recall…? Which is true or false?	Memory games and quizzes. Drill and practice/question and answer sessions. Describe the main character.
Comprehension	Classify Contrast Compare Discuss Illustrate Predict	What do you think…? What was the main idea? Briefly outline_____ Provide an example_____	Cut out or draw pictures to show a particular event. Write a summary. Prepare a flow chart to show the sequence of events. Draw a Venn diagram that compares and contrasts items/objects.
Application	Apply Calculate Change Choose Solve Modify	How could you illustrate_____? What examples can you find to _____? Do you know another instance where _____?	Write a diary entry as e.g. another person/from an animal's perspective. Make a photo essay of event/phenomena. Write a letter from a number of viewpoints.
Analysis	Analyse Conclude Criticise Categorize Differentiate Question	How is _____ related to_____? Why do you think _____? What ideas justify_____? If_____ happened, what might the ending have been?	Design a questionnaire to gather information. Put on a play about the area being studied. Identify a problem and identify causes and effects. Make a mind map.
Synthesis	Arrange Adapt Develop Substitute Modify Improve	How would you improve_____? How effective are _____? How would you adapt _____ to make a different _____?	Write about your feelings in relation to_____. Illustrate knowledge on a topic by composing a song to an already know melody. Debate a current issue – pros and cons.
Evaluation	Argue Assess Predict Summarise Rank Rate	How would you feel if___? Based on what you know, how would you explain_____? Prove or disprove_____.	Conduct a debate about an issue. What's it like to be_____? Design a board game that explains the process of_____.

Reflective Notes

Prior to reading this chapter, when you've planned professional development offerings, did "challenge" and "engage" play into your planning? If they did not, now is the time to begin. Incorporate the elements of challenging and engaging your team by planning activities and strategies before the actual professional development session, engagement activities during the session, and avenues of continued engagement and challenges after the session. Remember that professional development is continuous and should build on a subject matter and/or content area. What steps are you going to employ to ensure you challenge and engage your team during this learning process?

1.

2.

3.

4.

5.

6.

7.

Additional items I want to remember and employ to further challenge and engage my team/staff:

_____
_____
_____
_____

Meeting the new demands of standards-based reform will mean schools must not only change their approach to student learning, but to educator's learning as well.

CHAPTER 6
Accountability and Evaluation

Professional development can no longer just focus on exposing teachers to a concept or providing basic knowledge about a teaching methodology. Instead, professional development in an era of accountability requires a change in a teacher's practice that leads to increases in student learning.

The goal of all accountability systems is, or should be, the improvement of instruction and student learning. Accountability systems will foster improvement to the extent that they generate information relevant to teaching and learning and motivate teachers to use that information and work to improve practice.

As accountability within the constraints of schools/child development centers and other educational institutions are rising, accountability measures for the information received at professional development sessions are also rising. Accountability serves several purposes and has at its core the following questions:

- Who is accountable?
- To whom are they accountable?
- For what are they accountable?
- And with what consequences?
- By what standards? Measures?

As educators attend PD offerings and return to their original educational institutions, administrators should question as to the content received, the effects of such, the takeaways, and behavioral changes they will employ. For many, the training is just that—training. However as you continue to read, you will discover the best practices for holding your team accountable for every aspect of training received from that of morning connections, to networking opportunities, to content delivered via the facilitator, to hands-on activities, and of course, evaluations.

Coupled with training is that of evaluation and its connection to professional development. There are several reasons why the evaluation of professional development has become increasingly important. The first and foremost reason is accountability of services to the stakeholders and the children within the teacher's purview. This includes accountability of how we gain new knowledge and how that knowledge is used in practice; both of which involve processes, systems, and products.

Good evaluations don't have to be complicated. They simply require thoughtful planning, the ability to ask good questions, and a basic understanding of how to find valid answers. What's more, evaluations can provide meaningful information you can use to make thoughtful, responsible decisions about the professional development processes and its effects.

Evaluation design should be determined by the purpose for the evaluation—to improve or judge something. The evaluation process should begin in the planning stages and be based on clarity of thought regarding outcomes, the adult learning processes implemented, and the evidence required to guide effective decision making. Evaluations ask and answer significant questions, gather both quantitative and qualitative information from various vantage points and sources, and provide details as to recommendations and implementation strategies effecting future trainings.

Many administrators understand the importance of evaluation for event-driven professional development activities, such as workshops and seminars, but forget the wide range of less formal, ongoing, job-embedded professional development activities such as: study groups, action research, collaborative planning, curriculum development, structured observations, peer coaching, mentoring, and so on. But regardless of its form, professional development evaluation should be a purposeful endeavor.

If staff development is to improve student learning, many levels of change are required, each effective of its own particular evaluation challenges. Note that a great deal of staff development evaluations begin and end with the assessment of participants' immediate reactions to the training. While this data is important to collect for organizers and administrators, best practices references a design that also gathers information core to and beyond the initial questions of environment, facilitator knowledge level, handouts, and engagement opportunities.

An example of best practices questions reflects ones such as one's initial collection of data on participants' reactions, teachers' acquisition of new knowledge and skills, how the training affects teaching, and how those changes will affect student learning. Another question that is usually not included but will yield excellent notes and data is: How will the conducted training impact school culture and other organizational structures?

Effective professional development evaluations require the collection and analysis of four critical levels of information shown below (Guskey, 2000). With each succeeding level, the process of gathering evaluation information gets a bit more complex. And because each level builds on those that come before, success at one level is usually necessary for success at higher levels.

Evaluation Level	What Questions Are Addressed?	How Will Information Be Gathered?	What Is Measured or Assessed?	How Will Information Be Used?
1. Participants' Reactions	Was the subject presented appropriate? How will the knowledge attained be implemented? Was the content aligned to the goals/objectives? Were the objectives clearly stated? Was the leader knowledgeable? Helpful in terms of actionable items? Were refreshments offered? Rate the room (temperature, chairs, technology).	Questionnaires administered during breaks and at the end of the session. Comments collected via parking lots.	Initial satisfaction with the experience. Objective and goal achievement. Participants' participation.	To improve program design and delivery methods.
2. Participants' Learning	Did participants acquire the intended knowledge and skills?	Simulations Demonstrations Participant reflections (oral and/or written) Participant portfolios	New knowledge obtained and skills of participants.	To improve program content, format, delivery, and organization.
3. Organization Support Change	Was implementation advocated, facilitated, and supported? Were problems addressed quickly and efficiently? Were sufficient resources made available? Were successes recognized and	Questionnaires. Structured interviews with participants school administrators. Participant portfolios. Conversations with participants. Completion of assessments and evaluations.	The organization's advocacy, support, facilitation, and recognition.	To document and improve organizational support. To inform future change efforts. To incite discussion.

	shared? What was the impact on the organization? Did it affect the organization's climate and procedures?			
4. Participants' Use of New Knowledge and Skills	Did participants effectively apply the new knowledge and skills?	Questionnaires. Structured interviews with participants and their supervisors. Participant reflections (oral and/or written). Direct observations. Video- or audiotapes.	Degree and quality of implementation.	To document and improve the implementation of program content.

Level 1: Participants' Reactions

The first level of evaluation looks at participants' reactions to the professional development experience. This is the most common form of professional development evaluations, and the easiest type of information to gather and analyze. At Level 1, organizers address questions focusing on whether or not participants liked the experience. Did they feel their time was well spent? Were the activities well planned and meaningful? Was the leader knowledgeable and helpful? Did the participants find the information useful?

Important questions for professional development workshops and seminars also include: Were meals offered? Rate the room (temperature, chairs, technology). To some, questions such as these may seem inconsequential. But experienced professional developers know the importance of attending to these basic human needs.

Information on participants' reactions is generally gathered through questionnaires handed out at the end of a session or activity. These questionnaires typically include a combination of rating-scale items and open-ended response questions that allow participants to make personal comments. Because of the general nature of this information, many organizations use the same questionnaire for all their professional development activities; yet this is not one that is encouraged via best practices. To ensure the effectiveness of each session, evaluations should be specific and questions reflective of those surrounding room temperature, technology, etc., and should be tailored to meet the learning objectives and outcomes.

Level 2: Participants' Learning

Level 2 focuses on measuring the knowledge and skills participants gained over the PD session. Depending on the goals of the program or activity, this can involve anything from a traditional assessment to a simulation or full-scale skill demonstration. You can also use oral personal reflections or portfolios that participants assemble to document their learning.

Measures must show attainment of specific learning goals. This means that indicators of successful learning need to be outlined before each activity begins. Organizers can use this information as a basis for improving the content, format, and organization of the program or activities.

Level 3: Organization Support and Change

At Level 3, the focus shifts to the organization. Lack of organization support and change can sabotage any professional development effort.

Problems at Level 3 have essentially cancelled the gains made at Levels 1 and 2. That's why professional development evaluations must include information on organization support and change.

At Level 3, organizers should focus on questions about the organizational characteristics and attributes necessary for success. Did the professional development activities promote changes that were aligned with the mission of the school/company or organization? Were changes at the individual level encouraged and supported at all levels? Were sufficient resources made available? Were successes recognized and shared? Issues such as these can play a large part in determining the success of any professional development effort.

Gathering information at Level 3 is generally more complicated than at previous levels. Procedures differ depending on the goals of the program or activity. Additionally, organizers can use this information not only to document and improve organization support but also to inform future change initiatives and alignment with state, local, and national programs.

Level 4: Participants' Use of New Knowledge and Skills

At Level 4 evaluation questions are centered on: Did the new knowledge and skills participants gained make a difference in their practice? The key to gathering relevant information at this level rests in specifying clear indicators of both the degree and the quality of implementation. Unlike Levels 1 and 2, this information cannot be gathered at the end of a professional development session. Enough time must pass to allow participants to adapt the new ideas and practices. Because implementation is often a gradual and uneven process, you may also need to measure progress at several intervals.

In my practice, this is seen in an accountability form teachers complete at the end of their training sessions. The form is then given to literacy coaches and administrators for follow-up and observations. After a month, literacy coaches should follow up with teachers as to implementation procedures and questions stemming from the sessions, thus hindering successful transfer of knowledge or other items that are prohibiting knowledge to practice.

Routinely, coaching and peer mentoring are key in successful knowledge acquisition. It is also important to note that whenever I have a speaker or facilitator leading a session, I include in my initial conversations with the presenter a stipulation that he/she will be available for follow-up comments and/or guidance should the need arise for a designated period of time. This is a price structure I include in my budgets but have found to be of great benefit as teachers implement concepts and are in need of additional support measures. Please note that I do not have teachers themselves contact the facilitator; but I do expect for our literacy coaches and myself to have this access and then determine the necessary follow-up measures.

Teachers enrolled in our program note that on any given occasion they may be asked to share their professional development journals, be videotaped, and/or participate in peer-to-peer or other types of evaluation to ensure a transfer of knowledge. The negotiable and non-negotiable I referenced earlier in the book are also applicable here.

Professional development evaluations must take into account each stakeholder's needs in regard to data needed to effectively synthesize their training and its impact. Additionally, the tool must ensure the stakeholders have the prerequisites, knowledge, and skills to interpret and use the results effectively and appropriately.

Reflective Notes

Accountability and evaluation are essential elements of professional development trainings. Please reflect on the accountability measures you have in place to ensure teachers are implementing best practices and the knowledge gained from training sessions. Also notate your rating of your current evaluation tools. Are your tools antiquated, need revising, or are they meeting your needs to train and plan for supplemental sessions?

1.
2.
3.
4.
5.
6.
7.

Additional notes on the importance and incorporation of accountability and evaluations you want to remember/employ:

_____
_____
_____
_____
_____
_____
_____
_____

An ideal professional development climate has a non-threatening, non-judgmental atmosphere in which adults have permission for and are expected to share in the responsibility for their learning.

CHAPTER 7

Stimulating Environment

I was not sure what to expect as I entered the training today. For a month now I have heard that our professional development training was being reorganized to ensure teacher accountability and effectiveness, but I never thought it would also include the environment. As I entered the training, I saw white boards, chart paper, a well-designed and organized plan of thought, and commitment to both group and individual learning.

On each table were pads, pens, small manipulatives, and some treats. In the rear of the room appeared the learning objectives posted in clear language and numbered as to importance. On another wall I saw a list of terms. I found out later this was the pertinent terminology that would be used in the training. After a few minutes and a few pastries, the presenter began the training by introducing the learning objectives and then by assigning groups, partners, and communities. Each of these were used to reinforce strategies and concepts as well as to create a professional learning community.

This introduction was like no other and served as a foundation as what became the norm at all of our trainings. Each month; however, we all raced in to discover the environment and the lessons planned to ensure we understood what was being taught.

Many thanks to Dr. Rena for her commitment to excellence and dedication to RTS teachers. We are blessed to have her and this level of detail to our learning community. —Ms. Pleasant

Support for adult learners should be provided through a learning environment that meets both their physical and psychological needs. Such a learning environment is also an essential element in successful partnerships between learners and instructors. Developing an atmosphere in which adults feel both safe and challenged should be the goal.

Any anxieties learners might have about appearing foolish or exposing themselves to failure should be eased, but they should not feel so safe that they do not question their current assumptions or are not challenged in other ways. Instructors need to balance being friendly with challenging learners. An ideal adult learning climate has a non-threatening, non-judgemental atmosphere in which adults have permission for and are expected to share in the responsibility for their learning.

Professional development sessions should trigger the senses, facilitate independent learning, and maximize performance, ensuring that adults get the most out of training. As a facilitator, you'll want to identify your own preferred learning style and the styles of others, and discuss how to design training that appeals to all types of learners. Training tools and techniques should include: using metaphors, analogies, and stories; asking questions that promote learning; creating the right training atmosphere; and using memorable summaries and reviews.

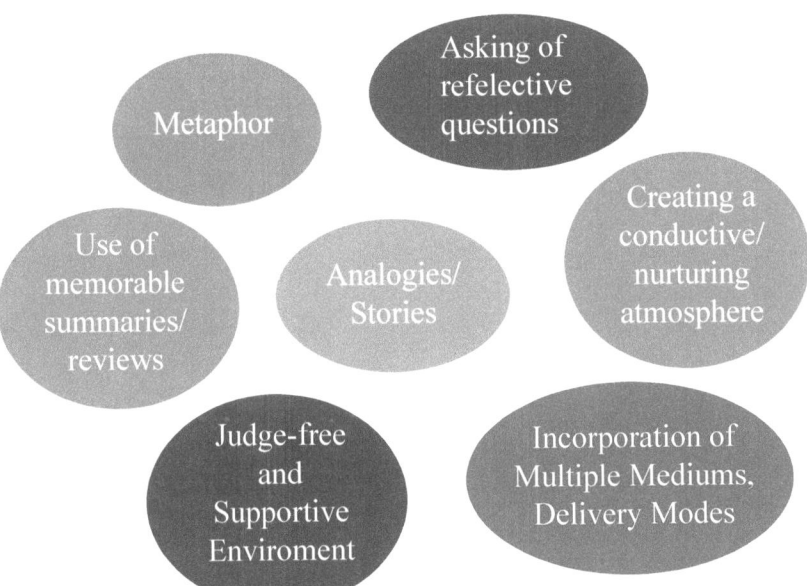

Suggestions for creating a learning environment that fosters a sense of support for and partnership with adults include the following:

- **Capitalize on the First Session.** First impressions are frequently lasting ones. The first session should create the foundation for a healthy learning partnership and set the tone for remaining sessions. Consider informal furniture arrangements with chairs in a circle or around a table and allow time for introductions, including information about the instructor. If the planned offerings are centered on those associated with learning communities or multiple sessions, it is imperative that a large portion of the first session be devoted to needs assessment and discussing learner expectations.

- **Incorporate Group Work.** Well-designed group work can contribute to the development of a collaborative, participatory learning environment in which the instructor is perceived as a partner. Small group activities foster the development of positive peer relationships among learners, which frequently have a much greater influence on learning than teacher-learner relationships. Informal, spontaneous groups can be used for short-term activities such as brainstorming. Groups can also be formed around ongoing projects. Formal, ongoing groups often result in stronger affiliation among members of the small group than among members of the whole class.

- **Break the Traditional Classroom Routine.** Deviating from the conventional practices associated with classrooms can help create an effective adult learning environment. A meal or snacks during a class break can create opportunities for interaction and break down barriers between instructors and learners. For trainings that meet more than five times, varying the meeting place can help add interest. Before changing the class meeting location; however, all participants should be consulted to ensure the change does not conflict with any existing arrangements for transportation and childcare.

Several of the sessions I conducted have rotated from location to location. While this presented some logistical issues, on average participants welcomed the opportunity to not only house trainings but also to showcase their center/school. The benefit is one where learning objectives were met as well as curiosity planted as to the new environment and ability to share best practices/tips as classrooms and environments were discussed and toured. A location change also erased some of the routine monotony of the trainings.

- **Support Opportunities for Individual Problem Solving.** Adults have many responsibilities besides that of learner and consequently may feel a sense of isolation in their student role. If appropriate, facilitators can encourage the formation of study groups (another opportunity for group work) to link those learners who may wish this type of support.

- **Room Décor.** Walking into a room where the intentionality of the organizer was that of reflective thought, attention to detail, and those of crafting a nurturing and sensory environment is my idea learning space. This sort of space is one I create for all of my professional development offerings. Whether it's black tablecloths, flowers on the tables or thoughtful centerpieces, purposeful notes along the wall etc., educators and administrators alike will know and understand my intent was to create a nurturing and warm environment.

Conductive and stimulating environments erase barriers, make those dreading the training feel a little more comfortable, foster discussion, participation, and excitement. Creating a theme and coordinating décor is not simply event planning but its core to facilitation and sensory attributions. The best reaction I can have at a PD experience is when participants arrive and they begin to manipulate the items I have placed on tables, to smell the flowers, and to circle the room, reading and charting on the paper or posters I have displayed.

This indulgence screams participation and being in tune with their environment. It is an organizer's dream come true and is a great tool for facilitators as these items can be used throughout the trainings to triangulate learning and foster robust discussions. Oftentimes the items themselves have already incited discussions, thoughts, and comments. Make this a part of your plan and ask about first impressions as part of your connecting activities.

> *Each training I organize and implement has a theme. The rooms are then transformed to reflect this theme. For Christmas it's stockings, Christmas boxes/snowmen, or trees. In the springtime it's fresh flowers and the beautiful spring colors; and fall trainings are similarly adorned in fall colors. Each training houses flip charts, special sayings, or focal points I can use to reconvene my group, to discuss their thoughts, and use to pair teams. One's environment is another tool that should complement the training from all aspects—temperature to décor. When possible, I ask participants for their input as to next month's themes, but I also carve out a surprise element.*

- **Elbow Room.** Oftentimes when trainings are being conceived, it is anticipated the masses will come. We place participants at tables or in groups/theatre seating elbow to elbow without room to wiggle, raise arms, or by gosh ... cough. This sort of arrangement does not facilitate a participatory environment except for the grappling as to table space. Best practices are aligned with relaxed meeting spaces that allow for ease in movement, one's ability to transition from a seating space to a standing space with ease and without interruptions, the movement of groups without worry as to noise and space, and the integration of experiential opportunities. As an organizer, I understand the importance of training to the masses, especially if budgets are an issue. However, I also understand the importance of quality training, thus reflective of "quality vs. quantity" mentality.

- **The Takeaway.** What is the takeaway you want your attendees to leave with? Is it the conference bag material? Room décor? Their experience? Conversations? Learning objectives? Implementation strategies, etc.? Whatever these are for you (hopefully a combination), the results should be communicated with participants. The takeaway should be that the environment was conductive to learning, their needs were supported, and they felt as if the training was implemented in a fashion that fostered understanding and promoted growth. If the aforementioned items are aligned, the items such as learning objectives, goal attainment, and the creation of learning support structures will be mastered and mastered well.

An additional best practice for creating simulating environments includes the shuffling of seating arrangements and the adding in of unexpected experiential engagements and thought provoking conversations. Laid (2000) documented the following which I also include in sequential trainings:

Supporting sequential sessions and providing a layer of surprise and movement to your training is best practice. Even if the activities of the learning session do not require changing the seating rearrangements, here are several reasons to do so:

o Learners are given a new perspective on the activity by sitting in a different part of the room.

o They become better acquainted with their peers.

o Learners are not consistently disadvantaged by being at greater distances from the screen/speakers.

o Small cliques do not arise—there is nothing wrong with cliques but in some cases they can become a problem by forcing their norms or agendas upon the entire group.

The following seating designs hit some of the pros and cons of different learning learning rooms:

Note: In the following seating arrangements, 0 = the learners, x = the trainer, and -- equals a table.

TRADITIONAL SEATING ARRANGEMENTS

```
           x
       0 0 0 0 0 0 0
       0 0 0 0 0 0 0
       0 0 0 0 0 0 0
       0 0 0 0 0 0 0
       0 0 0 0 0 0 0
```

o Best used for short lectures to large groups
o Communication tends to be one way (facilitator led)
o Facilitator cannot see the participants in the back (lack of engagement/eye contact)

Modified Traditional

```
           X
    O O O O   O O O O
    O O O O   O O O O
    O O O O   O O O O
    O O O O   O O O O
    O O O O   O O O O
```

- o Promotes participation
- o Allows the facilitator to see all the participants
- o Reduces space between facilitator and participants as facilitator can move up/down aisle
- o Best used for short lectures to large groups

Horseshoe

```
         X
      O     O
      O     O
      O     O
      O O O O O
```

- o Non-verbally encourages participation by allowing eye contact between the facilitator and all the participants
- o The facilitator is able to engage each participant
- o Works well when all participants must be able to see a demonstration
- o Perfect format for large group discussions

Modular

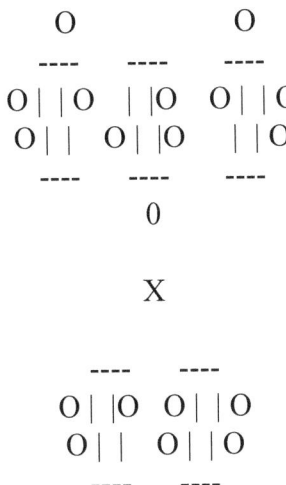

- Perfect for sessions involving group work or intense communications/discovery. The modular setting is great for professional learning communities as it keeps communities together while allowing for larger group discussions and explorations
- Allows facilitator to move between groups during lectures and activities
- Communication between facilitator and participants may be more difficult; this can be overcome via movement by the facilitator and the remembrance to check in often as to understanding, goals, objectivities etc.

CIRCLE

```
O O
O   X
O   O
O   O
O   O
O O
```

o Most democratic and unencumbered with no status symbol
o With no table each person is "totally revealed"
o Subtle nonverbal communications are possible
o Good for T-groups and sensitivity training (T-group trainings are those used when promoting communications or interpersonal skills)

** There will be conversations, shorter inputs, and more members will participate when they sit at a round table rather than at a square table

SQUARE

```
      Solid              Hole in middle

      O O O O            O X O O
      ----------         ----------
      O|      |O         O|------|O
      O|      |O         O||    ||O
      O|      |O         O||    ||O
      O|      |X         O|------|O
      ----------         ----------
      O O O O            O O O O
```

o More formality than a circle
o Depending where visual aids are placed, one side may become the "head of the table"
o A solid table normally encourages more conversation
o Tables with a hole in the middle tends to make some people less talkative, while encouraging others to speak for longer periods of time

RECTANGLE

```
         O O O O O
         ----------------
         O|         |O
         O|         |O
         ----------------
         O O x O O
```

o The seats at the short dimensions of the table are often seen as leadership positions
o If used, the participants should be forced to take distinctly different positions every now and then (i.e. randomly shift the name cards)

Scatter-Shot

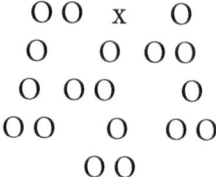

- o May appear haphazard but good for experiential training
- o Permits quick change of participant's focus
- o Produces tremendous investments of participant energy
- o Works well with multiple role plays
- o Participants can quickly form into large groups

Reflective Notes

The creation of a stimulating environment fosters a sense of support for a partnership with colleagues, provides insight as to the organization/district, and allows for individual growth. Are your professional development offerings in alignment with these offerings? Identify ways in which you can enhance your offerings, thus support to your team.

1.
2.
3.
4.
5.
6.
7.

Additional notes for consideration and remembrance as to the environment and its role in professional development trainings:

_____
_____
_____
_____
_____
_____
_____
_____

Teacher Professional Learning Logic Model
Excerpts from Haslam

A logic model is a graphical depiction of how a program intends to operate (program theory). Typically, program stakeholders work with evaluators to develop a shared understanding of a program. Logic models help clarify program activities, describe how those activities lead to certain outcomes, and ultimately how those outcomes link to program goals. Often, a logic model is used as a tool to stimulate discussion about program activities and outcomes that can help map out evaluation activities.

A logic model should be read from left to right, where more immediate resources and activities appear on the left and more distant outputs and outcomes appear on the right. It should be noted that all logic models are living documents that can change with the maturation of a program. It is expected that a logic model is updated as changes to a program occur. Another important point is that a logic model is a simplified depiction of a program. A logic model often fits on one page and is one dimensional, thereby missing some of the important aspects of a program.

Plan	Implement PD Trainings	Assess Formative Outcomes	Implement PD Trainings	Access Summative Outcomes
• Needs Assessment • Survey Teachers' Learning Styles • Identify Outcomes • Identify Location • Build Evaluations • Determine Resources Design PD	• Presentations • Workshops • Book Studies • Lending Libraries • Curriculum Planning • Peer Coaching	• New Knowledge and Skills Obtained • Teacher Perceptions • Change in Practice • Change in Organization • Change in Student Learning	• Presentations • Workshops • Book Studies • Learning Communities • Coaching	• Teacher perceptions • New knowledge and skills • Deeper change in practice/ • Deeper change in organization • More substantial change in student learning

Professional Development Standards
Excerpts from the National Staff Development Council

Professional development that improves the learning of all students prepares educators to apply research to decision making.

RESEARCHED-BASED

Professional development that improves the learning of all students uses learning strategies appropriate to the intended goal.

DESIGN

Professional development that improves the learning of all students prepares educators to understand and appreciate all students, creates orderly, safe, and supportive learning environments while promoting and holding high educational attainment.

EQUITY

Professional development that improvises the learning of all students deepens educators' content knowledge, provides them with research-based instructional strategies to assist rigorous academic standards, and prepares them to use various types of classroom assessments appropriately.

QUALITY TEACHING

Professional development that improves the learning of all students provides educators with knowledge and skills to involve families and other stakeholders appropriately.

FAMILY ENGAGEMENT

Professional development that improves the learning of all students uses multiple sources of information to guide improvement and demonstrate impact.

EVALUATION

Professional development that improves the learning of all students requires resources to support adult learning and collaborations.

RESOURCES

Seven Pitfalls

Introduction to Pitfalls

Planning and Preparations
Change
Delivery Methods
Learning Materials/Evaluations/Terminology
Unrealistic Expectations
Empty Vessels
Implementation Dip

Good teachers want to be great teachers. But no one—not even the most ardent supporters or detractors of tenure—can argue that many teachers are not getting the support and training they need to be effective and efficient in many of today's classrooms. According to a 2009 national research report, when asked about their experience in professional development, "most of those teachers … reported that it was totally useless" (Strauss, 2014).

For the most part, improving schools is ultimately about improving student performance. Contrary to popular thought, student achievement is not tied directly to higher expectations, more accountability, high-stakes tests, more time on task, new curricula and materials, more computers, or sophisticated lab equipment. Improved student performance is the result of improved teaching skills focused on average students (Hull, 2015). Hull continued by stating that traditional teacher preparation, as we have experienced it in this country, is tied to the behaviors, interests, and learning styles of the top students, i.e., the relatively small number of students who learn abstract concepts easily when taught by teachers who lecture but provide little in the way of application.

The problem to date has not been a lack of professional development opportunities per se. To the contrary, professional development for teachers has been included in every major initiative designed to improve student performance. The problem is that the quality of those programs has been inconsistent, and there has been no consensus on what constitutes quality. Many professional development activities stop short of producing their intended results. They point out problems with traditional teaching but offer little help in changing what happens in the classroom and provide no opportunities for participants to practice what they learn.

Seven Reasons Why Professional Development Sessions Fail

- The professional development content is inappropriate as it is general in nature and not supportive or relevant to their audiences' work (elementary vs. secondary vs. pre-kindergarten vs. state, federal, and district).

- Trainings are inappropriate in size, scope, or structure to support learning new ideas or skills. Gathering one hundred teachers into one room for a training event will never give them the time they need to reflect on the material, ask questions, listen to their peers, or go through activities to enhance their comprehension.

- The style of the professional development doesn't meet participants' learning needs; lecture oriented or completely experiential.

- Participants have been coerced or forced into the professional development.

- Lack of support for teachers' implementation of new instructional practices. Research shows there's an implementation gap in teachers' professional development. They may learn, understand, and agree with a new idea or technique presented in a workshop, but it's hard for them to implement that idea without ongoing support.

- There is little opportunity to interact with the material and discuss the ideas being presented, and little to no follow-up opportunities created.

- Participants in the session have personal problems or concerns that interfere with their ability to learn during the professional development offering.

Unfortunately for many teachers today professional development is seen more as a compliance exercise than a learning activity—and one where they have little if any choice. Fewer than one in three teachers reportedly chose most or all of their professional development opportunities as reported via the Bill & Melinda Gates Foundation (2014). Much of what systems consider professional development, educators perceive as wasted time. Therefore attention to planning and reflection opportunities will avoid pitfalls associated with lackluster trainings and those designed to fill the bill per se.

Twenty is the number of hours studies have cited as mandatory to ensure adequate training, instruction, and practice before a new teaching strategy is mastered and adequately implemented.

CHAPTER 1

Planning and Presentation

Professional development can succeed only in settings or contexts that support it. The most critical component of that support must flow from administrators/center directors. The outcome of every professional development initiative will depend ultimately on whether its administrators consider it important; thus their support and allegiance to the time, progress, and interactions. For this reason, buy-in on the part of administrators is a critical first step to success.

It's Monday morning at 9:30 a.m. and we just realized next Monday is President's Day. (Since the state is closed, this is the perfect time to schedule teacher PD). It's a week out ... but I think we can do this. So the planning begins. Paper and pens are secured as the plan is devised. Let's call the state and have first aid training. Then we can add in child abuse training; after which we can talk about communication procedures and individualized instruction. That's a total of seven hours, which leaves roughly thirty minutes for lunch. It's a plan—let's notify teachers.

The above situation is one I hear often and have been called upon to relieve stress when planning begins, at the last minute, and with little knowledge of actual participants' needs and an understanding of the overall goal and objectives of the PD session. While I am quite aware of the state and/or districts' demands to implement PD, I know from experience that poorly designed, facilitated, and implemented professional development sessions stifle one's experience and negate the learning process.

Another characteristic of a pitfall that inadvertently hampers professional development is when administrators and teachers alike are unprepared or unwilling to change their thought processes or interactions that a well-designed professional development training should foster. (Such was the case I referenced earlier as to the training I facilitated in the northern part of the US) Before change can take place there must be a shared sense or need for change—the more strongly and widely felt the better. For example, simply telling teachers their students' oral language acquisition skills are low is not enough to generate the sense of urgency that instructional change requires.

Planning and preparation is equally critical for both presenters and attendees. If a presenter is ill-prepared, they are not going to be engaging and prepared to address the varied personalities and experiences of attendees. Additionally, this lack of preparedness will be manifested in the manner in which the session is implemented via lectures and activities. When attendees are ill-prepared, they are basically there to sign in and obtain their certificates (most often this is the case for many educators). Attendees with this mentality will be hard to engage and may be prepared to disprove the presenter's theories and concepts by a distain for the PD session or lack of willingness to participate in the overall day. Several studies revealed that teacher unpreparedness results in the leadership or organizers' neglect to correctly inform as to the topics, rationale for attendance, and expectations upon completion of the training. Educators are also trying to determine the subject matters' relevance to their jobs/classrooms, and depending on this, suffer attitude conflicts and disengagements regarding the training.

Planning and preparation are also noted as barriers when teachers and administrators alike identify a number of professional development experiences that hinder or stifle learning. These barriers are associated with insufficient time, lack of financial resources to pay for professional development, learning that is not customized to the content being taught and the skills needed to be developed, as well as a lack of continuity between professional development sessions. Educators also site administrators as integral in the pitfall domain as they often are not supportive and are negligent when approving substitutes and schedules changes.

The fragmented nature of the professional development market also serves as a pitfall. Of the $18 billion spent annually on professional development, only $3 billion is delivered by external providers. The vast majority of professional development spending represents internal investments by local school districts and outside community organizations who have placed a stake in the ground concerning education and its impact on communities. To this end, professional development does not work like a typical market in which the best products are as well known by its users and gain an increasing share over time. Professional development is not subject to market analysis at all, as the purchasers are also the suppliers (Gates, 2014).

To avoid planning pitfalls, use the checklist below for optimal design:

What is the need (specific training or focus area; teachers/school/center/organization)?	
How do you know the training is needed?	
Desired outcomes	
Learning opportunity/including practice and coaching	
Available and potential resources	
Duration/time frame of training Formative/summative evaluations	
Avenues to expand upon the learning opportunities	
Next steps in the process	

Pesky pitfalls of professional development offerings are alive and well. The following key questions should be considered when planning, as they will aid in optimal planning and delivery:

- What are your goals (session, yearly, teacher specific)?

- What do your student data and needs assessment reveal about our training needs?

- Are the selected topics for training aligned with the district's grade-level plan and scientifically based research?

- Who is our target audience?
- How much has been allocated in the budget for training?
- Are there sufficient funds to cover all related expenses (e.g., location, presenters, materials etc.)?
- How does this training align with existing professional development opportunities?
- How can other stakeholders (e.g., higher education faculty or business partners) be involved in the implementation of the plan?
- How many presenters are needed and who will be responsible for communicating with them about training needs and logistics?
- Are the presenters qualified to conduct the sessions?
- Where and when will the session(s) be held?
- What materials are needed? How much is needed?
- How will new or reassigned teachers have access to the information after the initial training?
- Who will be responsible for securing the location and presenters and for notifying participants?
- How often and by whom will follow-up be provided?

While the above seems like a lot of questions to answer, the data generated will yield a successful professional development offering meeting each of your attendees' needs and will aid in the establishment of your goals and objectives. Furthermore, your evaluation will speak volumes, as it should be created in tandem with the questions you are posing, thus a true indication of your PD offering and its impact.

The most important concept to remember when planning and communicating professional development is that PD offerings are a continuous process and should follow a continuum in which educators or participants will grow in their skill attainment and job relevance. This is a perfect time to start with the end in mind, or as I referenced earlier in the book—implement-backwards planning.

Reflective Notes

Prior planning prevents poor performances. How can you ensure your professional development opportunities are planned to meet your team's needs and engage at an optimal level?

1.
2.
3.
4.
5.
6.
7.

Additional notes referencing planning pitfalls:
_____
_____
_____
_____
_____
_____
_____
_____
_____
_____
_____
_____

Professional learning that increases educator effectiveness and results for all students applies research on change and sustains support for implementation of professional learning and creates environments for long-term change.

CHAPTER 2

Change

C-H-A-N-G-E ... six small but powerful letters that in most people invoke feelings of fear, insecurity, and harbor stress; sometimes to the point of becoming ill or engaging in the act of retreating. Change presses us out of our comfort zone and forces us to see the boundaries beyond our current view. Change is inequitable, not a respecter of person. Depending on your advantage point, **CHANGE** is slated as for "better" or "worse."

Over the past twenty years, I have had the pleasure of changing my life every three years as we relocated to support Kent's military deployment. Change became a way of life for us, although not one accepted easily and without resistance. I remember our first move to Green Bay, WI. "Who lives in Green Bay?" I remember questioning. At this point, Jonathan, our youngest, was six months old and all I could think about was my family and support structure, and of course, the unknown. What would I do if Kent were deployed while there? What if there was an emergency? What? What? What?

As we settled in, I remember meeting families upon families in my same situation who became support structures and extended families for each other. I also realized that CHANGE has it positives and provided our family with opportunities we would not have otherwise experienced, such as living abroad for three years and traveling to countries I could have only dreamed.

I must note that while I accepted the change, this was not my first choice. Like many, I cried, tossed, and turned at night, and complained to the point of no return. Then I drank a cup of tea and decided I needed to accept this opportunity as a gift and thus prepare my family. Each rotation as we moved, I made the kids read Who Moved my Cheese? As I wanted them to adequately prepare for the transition and to realize they had to, and most importantly be, a participant of the change and not a bystander.

Change is not a new concept for educators; education has been in the business of change for decades. Over the past several decades the questions of change and its impact has been studied for years. Questions such as "How and why do individuals change their crafts?" "Why do people resist change?" and "Why do adults change?" are a few questions at the heart of the educational debate. Change is not manifested in individuals alone as organizational structures must adhere to the proposed changes and must also support and encourage the change often acting as more of a change agent to ensure complete transformation.

In the professional development arena, change conjures up a lot of emotions and drives fear as to the "What-if's" or "Why." To create consistent and sustained change, the system/districts/organizations and their administrators should initiate, implement, and maintain the desired change for it to become common practice and to create conditions in which to foster the change and associated growth.

Pitfalls are noted in the changes area as most often changes are told and explained later. This creates opportunity for one's or a team's own translations. CHANGE in the professional development area may also equate to the old practice as no longer effective or a new leader or person trying out their tactics or ideas without the voice of others. Also noted in the PD area is that of resistance to change. Such resistance can manifest in the form of sabotage and neglect for ongoing and supportive engagement, coaching, or completion of tasks/assignments designed to improve the environment.

To avoid pitfalls, change must be implemented well, with a high degree of fidelity; otherwise the change will not be sustained as it will live a half-hearted life and will eventually fade. One of the first steps of applying change is for administrators and districts to accept the course of action to be taken, to all agree as to the process and steps, and to communicate not only the steps of the process to their team but to also explain the rationale behind the change theory.

Learning Forward documents that effective professional development begins with the establishment of clear goals and high expectations for implementing the change with fidelity. Therefore, those responsible for professional development should apply steps to ensure the conflict associated with a new philosophy or practice will be listened to and properly discussed in a non-abrasive format, coupled with experiential learning opportunities and support structures already developed.

Research conducted states the stages of concern and the levels of use are integral in avoiding pitfalls of implementing and fostering change. Stages of concern as noted in Learning Forward describe the affective or personal dimensions of change, whether it's a school, classroom, or a person. Additionally, the stages provide a way to better understand and then address educators' common concerns as to the changes they are about to accept and are required to work within. The levels of use identified behaviors individuals employ when approaching change, such as those associated with fear, trust, attitudes, and perceptions.

The stages of concern are:

Stage 1	**Awareness** – Aware that innovation is being introduced but not really interested or concerned with the change.
Stage 2	**Informational** – Interested in obtaining information and understanding as to the change.
Stage 3	**Personal** – How will the change impact me personally?
Stage 4	**Management** – How will the change be managed as it is implemented/practiced?
Stage 5	**Consequences** – What is the impact of the change on students, implementation, organizations, and culture?
Stage 6	**Collaboration** – Will I work with others to ensure the change is implemented successfully?
Stage 7	**Refocusing** – Transformation begins as to refining the innovation to improve learning objectives.

In **Stage 1**, to avoid pitfalls, involve educators in discussions and decisions about the innovation and its implementation, framework, and expectations. Share only enough information at first to arouse interest, yet avoid portraying too much information as it could create overwhelming feelings and confusion. It is also important to acknowledge that questions and ambitiousness are expected and that you will work towards a solution together.

In **Stage 2**, provide clear and accurate information as to the innovation/change using several modalities across multiple time frames. It will be imperative here to assist educators in seeing how the change is relevant to their direct responsibilities and scope of work.

Stage 3, is critical to the process as it legitimizes personal feelings/emotions. This is a great opportunity for administrators to notate these conversations and provide enforcements and encouragement as to personal adequacy and support measures.

Stage 4, is concerned with the management of the concerns and aids in calcifying the steps and components of the innovation, providing answers that address small, specific, how-to issues and connecting teachers with others whose personal concerns have been diminished and are now supportive of the process.

Stage 5, encourages and diminishes the likelihood of consequences and occurrences as it provides opportunities that foster demonstrations of change/innovation in other settings where success has been accomplished. This is also where feedback and support on an individual level is warranted.

Stage 6, develops skills for working collaboratively, bridging both internal and external resources.

Stage 7, respects and encourages interest in individuals for agreeing to give the innovation a change in deciphering a better way to conduct business or impact change. This stage also assists educators in channeling their ideas and energies in a productive manner and offers an array of resources for use and exploration.

Simply stated, CHANGE is learning and learning produces CHANGE. In the professional development arena change is evoked and tested as new material and concepts are introduced and expected to be placed into practice. When teams/educators are supported and informed as to the upcoming or expected changes, transitions are made easily and are fostered in a manner that engages everyone.

To avoid the pitfalls of change, consistent, ongoing, and supportive teacher professional development should be employed and practiced routinely via the services of learning communities, coaches, evaluations, and reflections. Each time a person participates in any sort of PD offering, the administrators, organizers, etc., are anticipating or expecting some sort of change in behavior/design/attitude or approach; therefore reasonable expectations must be in place to support the participants in their new acquisition of knowledge.

Additional measures must be placed in practice to also aid the administrators so they know how to recognize the change, how to support it, and when to offer assistance, advice, and additional professional development offerings. Change, as stated by Fullan (2001), cannot be managed, but can be controlled and understood. Professional development facilitators, organizers, and participants equally must be mindful of this and recognize where they land on the issues and be open for additional and supportive measures.

Reflective Notes

CHANGE is difficult. Everyone within the organization/district/school is responsible for implementing some aspects of change to create a coherent, cohesive system that supports the team/participants. Describe methods you will employ to ensure change is presented in a successful manner and supported for optimal implementation.

1.
2.
3.
4.
5.
6.
7.

Additional notes referencing change you want to employ:
_____
_____
_____
_____
_____
_____
_____
_____

Professional development should focus on curricular and instructional strategies that have a high probability of affecting students' ability to learn.

CHAPTER 3

Delivery Methods

Traditional professional development trainings are not only largely ineffective at changing educators' practice, but is also an ineffective manner in which to convey theoretical concepts and evidence-based research.

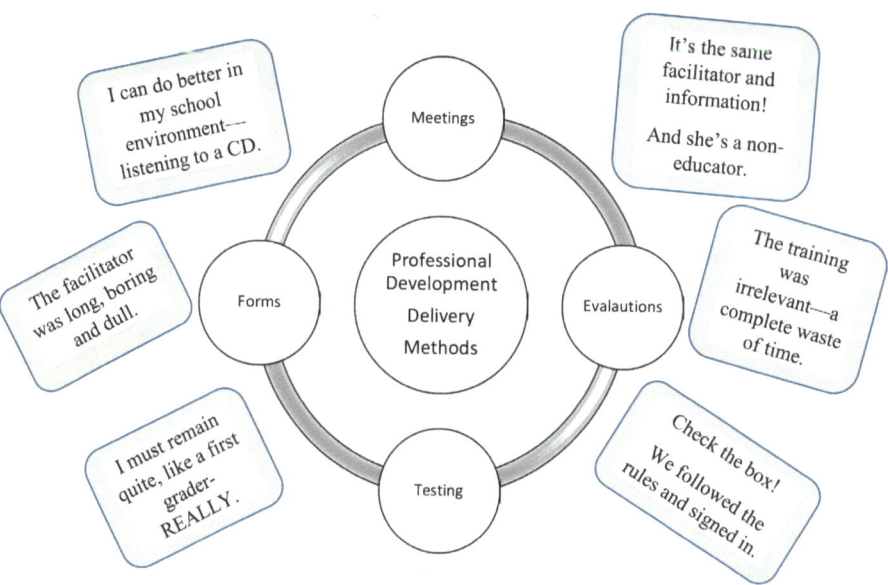

Traditional staff development opportunities for educators usually take the form of one-size-fits-all, one-day workshops. Administrators usually determine topics of focus. Teachers are expected to attend workshops in order to take away key understandings about teaching and learning or specific instructional methodologies and strategies they can employ in the classroom for immediate, positive results. The ideology behind traditional staff development opportunities seems rational and seems as though it yields positive results for teachers and students. However, many teachers find these workshops to be a waste of time because of the lack of correlation between their perceived needs as professionals and what is actually offered through staff development opportunities.

Lock (2006) highlights key issues that influence the level of impact professional development opportunities have on teaching and learning. First and foremost, most teachers find little value in one-size-fits-all, one-day workshops that are not connected to their current, everyday practices or experience. Furthermore, such workshops generally rely on transmission of knowledge from experts to teachers. Lock further asserts that traditional staff development opportunities fail to meet school-specific needs and do not provide sufficient time for teachers to plan or to effectively learn new teaching methodologies or strategies.

Pitfalls

Today, PD opportunities provide teachers with innovative and hands-on activities that facilitators are excited to introduce into the classroom. Yet these techniques and tips are oftentimes met with "Well, we don't do that here" or "That won't work with our kids." Therefore the robust nature and newfound skills are brushed into the memories basket and the old routines continue as status quo.

Teasing. Refrain from teasing teachers with tools they are not able to, encouraged, or allowed to use. Teachers like participating in insightful and innovative professional development with exciting methodologies, yet dislike it when administrators refuse to allow change or adaptations to the daily classroom activities or implementation structures. I can imagine the brutality of sending teachers back into the classroom after attending a resounding session filled with cutting-edge research and best practices. Quick fix: Ensure the contents and items covered are adequately discussed with administrators prior to obtain buy-in; garner comments and suggestions for stating access and implementation procedures.

One Size Fits All. This type of PD offering uses a single focus to address all attendees' learning styles as well as goals and objectives as communicated through the PD organizers. The one-size-fits-all approach is designed to meet all teachers by a standard delivery approach with mundane discussion and activities embedded.

Teachers often express that traditional professional development workshops lack a clear purpose and direct application to everyday classroom experience because these opportunities are rarely connected to the varying levels of teacher expertise and skill. Furthermore, many teachers feel the one-size-fits-all, one-day workshops do not sustain the types of critical conversations that need to happen frequently to encourage optimal professional growth.

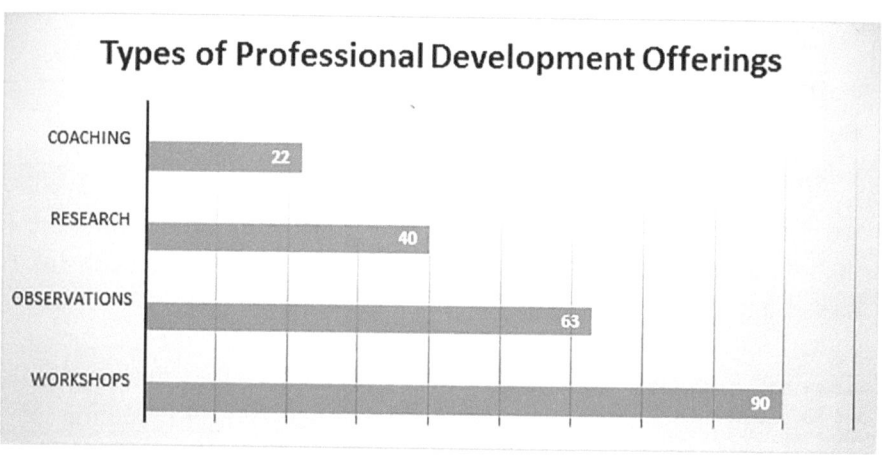

The worst PD offerings are those that are condescending and patronizing (like the one I referenced in the previous chapter). This most often occurs as the presenter is one who has not taught in years or those who have never taught. Either case, facilitation from these so-called experts easily allows for condescension creep. Because the world of education has changed, the manner in which we implement such and address our students' needs has also changed. Therefore, it is imperative to be mindful of the following routine activities of common PD offerings:

> The one-size-fits-all-offering is not effective...
>
> Refrain from telling me to differentiate if you are not modeling this during the session.

> Remind me to use inquiry-based learning as the center of my instruction when you only lecture during the session.

> Asking me to engage students via constructivist activities; yet your delivery modes are handouts and powerpoint.

Time is a component of the delivery method as research indicated that effective professional development requires a significant amount of teacher time. This finding is largely due to the fact that the learning curve for teachers is greatest at the implementation stage, when teachers need the most support as the new skill is practiced. Time is a pitfall as administrators alike consider this implementation time as unwanted in most cases as this should have been factored into the training phase; thus now teachers can be held accountable.

Coaching is a great resource and delivery mode of professional development when performed correctly. The goal of coaching is to ensure teachers possess the tools and skills needed to implement instruction to their potential and are effectively impacting instruction that yields results for students. Therefore, coaches must be well versed in not only their area of expertise but also in the art of coaching and its respective dynamics. For coaching to be delivered at an optimal level, therefore avoiding pitfalls, several components must be interwoven into the offering:

- **Competency lead** – By appreciating a teacher's current level of competence, coaches value the natural learning processes of those they coach. Encouraging teachers to clarify what they want and need, to build on their strengths, and to experiment in mutually agreed-on goals empowers them to take more initiative and responsibility for their own learning and professional development.

- **Ongoing** – Coaching must be ongoing two to three days a week to yield optimal results.

- **Delivery** – Coaching should be implemented using various delivery methods, such as side by side and demonstration.

- **Teacher-centered** – When conversations are coach centered, the coach's expertise has the upper hand. The coach demonstrates, advises, and teaches. The more knowledge the coach has, the more tempted he/she will be to take a coach-centered approach. Unfortunately, this often undermines learning: People don't resist change; they resist being changed. Thus the need to ensure coaching is performed through the teacher-centered approach.

> *In fact, I instruct our coaches to allow teachers to talk first and recap their concerns/challenges and acknowledge their success prior to the coach chiming in. This process allows educators to realize they have a voice and their voice matters. In fact, the teachers within our program have all commented that this process has enabled them to acknowledge their thoughts and feelings better and in some cases*

self-correct, knowing they are not being punished or held to higher standards. They also noted they are freer to document their findings and seek additional questions or support via their coach.

To facilitate learning, coaches must take off the expert hat, asking rather than telling, in order to assist teachers to adapt recommendations and find their own best way forward. Authentic coaching puts teachers at the center of their own professional learning. They own the process. They're animated, energized—and in charge.

- **Non-evaluative** – A common mistake is for administrators to link coaching with evaluations. When coaching conversations are high stakes, coaches have crossed the line into evaluation, watching and listening to analyze and correct what's wrong. Crossing that line is problematic when it comes to professional development. Assessing performance problems can trigger destructive patterns of faultfinding and finger pointing, regardless of how constructive the intentions of the coach may be. In the search for causes (what to blame), people too often find culprits (whom to blame). Internalizing such judgments can take a crippling toll on teacher self-efficacy and motivation (Moran, 2011).

  When teachers don't do as well as they would like, coaches need to listen carefully and express empathy to facilitate the release of negative emotions, which have been shown to have a detrimental effect on learning, creativity, and openness to change. Through empathetic listening, coaches reduce defensiveness and increase teacher engagement in their own professional development.

- **Strengths-based** – When conversations are deficit based the weaknesses of teachers have the upper hand. The focus is on problem areas that need to be fixed. Focusing on deficits also shifts the responsibility for learning to the coach, who presumably knows how to do things better. Strengths-based coaching starts with a different assumption: In every situation, no matter how bleak, something always works. By identifying those areas of positive practice, coaches help teachers to build self-efficacy, set self-directed learning goals, brainstorm strategies, and design ways of moving forward. By discovering and developing their strengths, teachers can transform their weaknesses without having to tackle them head-on (Moran, 2011).

I would be remiss if I did not state there is a huge difference between coaching and mentoring. In order for your coaching sessions to yield positive fruit, administrators and organizers alike need to clarify the roles and expectations of coaching, highlighting and ensuring that teachers understand coaches will serve as coaches—not mentors or counselors.

One-time offerings of professional development sessions are not adequate professional development models or philosophies or ones that will yield optimal results for staff. One-time offerings are great as kickoffs, jump starters, and bridges, but are ineffective as comprehensive behavioral change procedures. Therefore, organizers should be mindful to plan those one-time offerings in conjunction with their regular PD structure, using these as best practices, bridges, motivators, and hands-on opportunities to ensure implementation of a skill or practice after other PD measures have been practiced. Remember, professional development is a continuum and should operate not in a vacuum but in a synchronized approach to the learning, understating, and implementation of a goal/objective.

To avoid these pitfalls, consider the following to leverage and differentiate professional development:

1. How will participants' needs be identified?
2. Do participants' needs reveal patterns or trends?
3. How will participants be given the autonomy to expand their knowledge/skills?
4. Identify support structures already in existence.
5. What resources are needed to differentiate and implement various learning strategies?
6. How does differentiating work with collaborative learning?
7. How will you incorporate opportunities for deep, meaningful reflection and feedback?

Reflective Notes

Professional development opportunities should be continuous, multifaceted, and tailored to meet the participants' needs and professional goals. As you strive to avoid pitfalls during delivery, what steps are you going to implement and what items should you be mindful?

1.
2.
3.
4.
5.
6.
7.

What additional notes do you want to remember from the aforementioned section?

_____
_____
_____
_____
_____
_____
_____
_____

There is an undeniable truth that teaching is inherently complex and nuanced. Professional development must recognize and address this!

CHAPTER 4

Learning Materials, Resources & Terminology

Effective professional learning requires human, fiscal, material, technology, and time resources to achieve student-learning goals. How resources are allocated for professional learning can overcome inequities and achieve results for educators and students. The availability and allocation of resources for professional learning affect its quality and results. Understanding the resources associated with professional learning and actively and accurately tracking them facilitate better decisions about and increased quality and results of professional learning.

Resources for professional learning include staff, materials, technology, and time, all dependent on available funding. How these resources are prioritized to align with identified professional learning needs affects access to, quality of, and effectiveness of educator learning experiences. Decisions about resources for professional learning require a thorough understanding of student and educator learning needs, clear commitment to ensure equity in resource allocation, and thoughtful consideration of priorities to achieve the intended outcomes for students and educators.

Staff costs are a significant portion of the resource investment in professional learning. Costs in this category include school and school system leaders and other specialized staff that facilitate or support school or school system-based professional learning, such as instructional coaches, facilitators, and mentors, as well as salary costs for educators when professional learning occurs within their workday. The time leaders commit to professional learning, either their own or for those they supervise, is a cost factor because it is time these leaders are investing in professional learning; managing this time is another area of responsibility for leaders.

Time allocated for professional learning is another significant investment. Education systems nationwide have schedules that provide time in the school day for teacher collaboration and planning to increase student learning. Learning time for educators may extend into after-school meetings, summer-extended learning experiences, and occasional times during the workday when students are not present.

Technology and material resources for professional learning create opportunities to access information that enriches practice. Use of high-speed broadband, Web-based, and other technologies, professional journals and books, software, and a comprehensive learning management system is essential to support individual and collaborative professional learning.

Pitfalls Learning material designed to enrich professional development offerings can sometimes present a negative effect when the material is presented with little forethought and prior communication. Learning materials can be varied, but each item must be carefully selected as to usage and connectedness to the learning objectives and goals.

Content associated with professional development must be strong in nature and measured for its robustness and adherence to brain-based research, Bloom's Taxonomy, and best practices. To be effective, professional development should be based on curricular and instructional strategies that have a high probability of affecting student learning and, just as important, students' ability to learn.

Generally, learning materials/opportunities consist of the following: (1) deepen teachers' knowledge of the subjects being taught; (2) sharpen teaching skills in the classroom; (3) keeping up with developments in one's field, and in education generally; (4) generate and contribute new knowledge to the profession; (5) increase the ability to monitor students' work in order to provide constructive feedback to students and appropriately redirect teaching; (6) innovative practices aligned with various instructional delivery modalities; and (7) supplies, material, and financial resources to support the incorporation of new practices/tools. Pitfalls arise if any of the above-mentioned elements are voided, not supported, misunderstood, or not evaluated as to implementation, relevance, and goal acquisition.

Professional development should always address identified gaps in student achievement. For example, it would be pointless to offer professional development to raise student performance in literacy if students are doing well in literacy but poorly in numeracy. The content of professional development should center on subject matter, measurement of student performance, and inquiry regarding professional questions that are relevant to the setting in which the professional development is delivered. By staying within this frame of reference, teacher professional development can focus on real issues and avoid providing information that may not benefit the participants; thus PITFALLS.

Resources

As I conducted research for this book, I noticed there were not a lot of documented resources materials needed to support the optimal delivery of professional development. Therefore, I conducted an evaluation of teachers and administrators with whom I have worked over the past five years. This research yielded there is a gap in services and communication as to expectations and teachers' ability to arrive at professional development offerings prepared and in ensuring that subsequent or follow-up sessions will further the previous offerings and support ongoing development.

Resources as noted by teachers/administrators surveyed are:

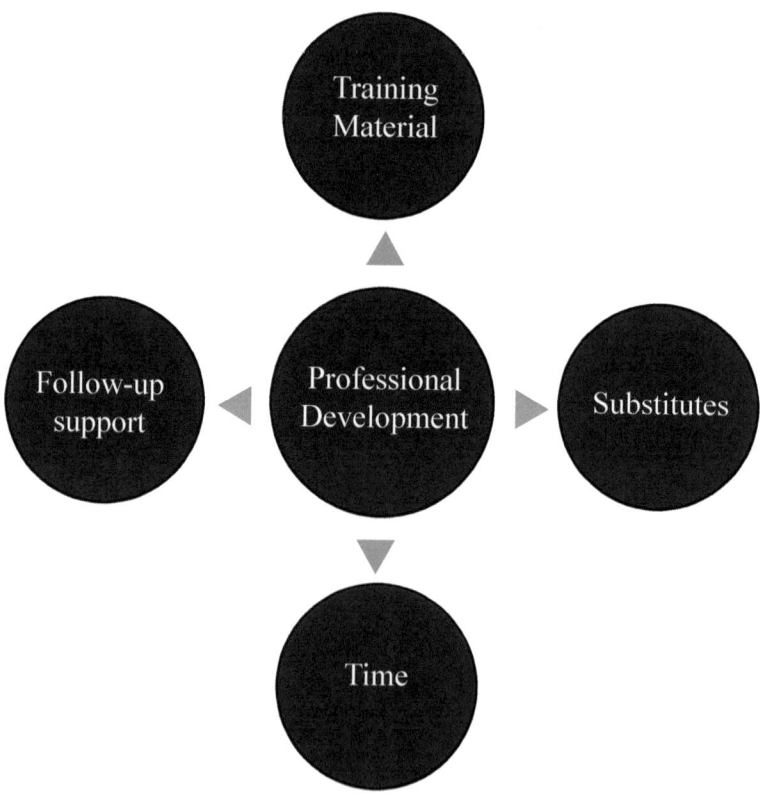

Training material equates to the amount of tools necessary to first of all attend the workshops, pens, papers, curriculum, implementation strategies, textbooks, access to digital devices and technology, in addition to student-specific items needed (calculators, microscopes, worksheets, books, panel cards, etc.). Having the material equates the full implementation of the content taught, thereby removing hindrances and obstacles deemed as preventive.

Utilizing substitutes is simply having access to coverage that allows engagement in professional development opportunities. Substitutes will be warranted for each type of engagement except for coaching opportunities in the classroom. Substitutes remove the potentiality for teachers having to worry as to classroom conduct, expectations being excited during the development time, as well as allow the clearing of the mind to intake new information and relate it to the content presented. As stated, substitutes should be warranted for all types of PD offerings as well as travel.

Time is of the essence as it reflects the timing needed to engage in PD, follow-up, and implementation time, as well as time for reflection and peer-to-peer time (study group, discussions/sharing of best practices/strategies, and work time). Time is also reflective of the time it takes to actually implement a content via impactful change. Timing includes time to explain the content and process to students, administrators, and fellow teachers, and for the implementation to feel comfortable. Timing also fosters introduction and implementation within the respective environments.

Teachers and researchers alike have discovered it takes roughly four to nine months to effect change in a positive manner and to actually see the results. Therefore, formative and summative evaluations should be factored into the timing phase and should also be noted as a factor when determining timing and successful implementation.

Follow-up support is reported as those being supplied and endorsed by administrators and are reflective of timing, supplies, ability to sit in and/or observe as fellow or neighboring teachers implement the newly taught content/best practices, as well as leaveway as additional research, questioning and assistance is obtained via coaches or professional learning communities.

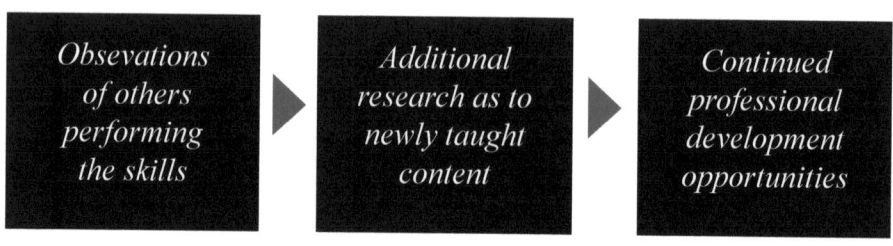

TERMINOLOGY

Pitfalls *FSPK and DLM curriculums associated within the GRFS program are all facets of a larger version of school reform and educational offerings offered via the school incentive program and thus provide support to the FRG with the utilitarian of the USACAPOC infrastructure. Did the unfamiliar terms depict meaning or render the passage null and void?*

Consistent terminology and definitions related to PD methods, roles, knowledge, and capabilities have emerged as a critical issue for the early education field. Recently, states have experienced new, early childhood education system challenges and needs related to training and technical assistance (TA). The urgency of these issues grows, particularly as states increase their focus and work on quality improvement activities, including quality rating and improvement systems (QRIS).

Terminology is an important connector when relaying meaning and establishing lines of effective communication. In fact, terminology is a core component of communication and is key when deciphering meaning and aiding in the understanding of concepts, clues, and text.

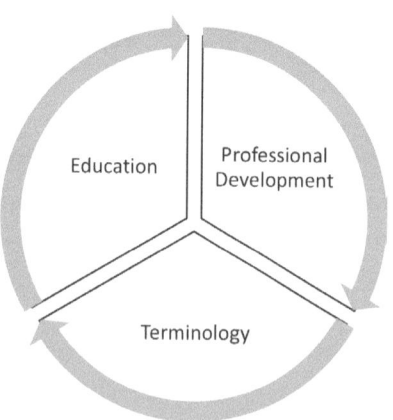

PD efforts, while important, have been hampered by irregular wording and inconsistent definitions. Staff use multiple terms to describe or provide a context for different forms of professional development. For example, many agencies use the terms "professional development" and "workshops" to mean the same thing, while others believe that workshops are one component of a larger professional development strategy.

Some organizations distinguish professional development, which enriches the individual, from staff development, which enriches the program or agency. Others use these terms interchangeably. Unfortunately, because this is no central portal, there is a void in the common reference point through which to synchronize educational terminology.

In a field such as education we shouldn't expect a great deal of variation in our definitions and terminology. Yet, because of the new wave of teachers and educational support teams/administrators, terminology is quite an issue and one requiring closer attention. Education relies on disciplines from various sectors to enhance the quality of instruction and in addressing student needs. These are evident through collaborations with external classrooms, social work services, child development centers, and support and recreational services.

Each of these entities has its own nomenclature, which further complicates the learning environment. Within the professional development setting these frames of reference are different for each participant, depending on their expertise and background, as well as the educational institution assigned. Note that I am referencing education here, but terminology is key in any sector and causes one to pause and take heed on terminology prior to implementing or facilitating a PD session.

Reflective Notes

Learning materials, resources, and terminology all work together to ensure optimal design and delivery of professional development offerings. Indicate below your thoughts as to these and the steps you will take to avoid pitfalls relating to each.

1.
2.
3.
4.
5.
6.
7.

Additional notes pertinent to avoiding pitfalls:

_____
_____
_____
_____
_____
_____
_____
_____
_____
_____

Professional development can no longer center on exposing teachers to a concept or simply providing basic knowledge about a specific methodology. Instead, during this era of teacher accountability, professional development requires a change in teachers' practices that lead to increases in student learning.

CHAPTER 5

Unrealistic Expectations

Yes we can! Yes we can have a two-day-long productive, professional development session that incorporates multiple intelligence, brain-smart tips, and hands-on activities, all while adhering to the tenets of adult learners. Yes, we can accomplish all of this. We only need to ensure that our teachers have a thirty-minute lunch break and have presenters set up to come in and train one after the other. And let's incorporate one morning break and one afternoon break to ensure we are meeting the needs of the teachers.

The day should being at 8 a.m. and end at 5 p.m., as this is our regularly scheduled workday (an excerpt taken from an administrators meeting in which I was asked to provide the keynote, direction, and reflection). The second day can be filled with paired classroom assessments and mini meetings with administrators. Sounds good—let's notify the team and talk to the cook to coordinate lunch and snacks.

The actual results of the aforementioned: Unresponsive teachers who failed to attain any of the learning goals and objectives and an administration team who looked at me wondering, What went wrong? The answer was simple: The administration team wanted to take advantage of their two-day in-service training. Instead of the training being focused and tailored to meet the needs of the teachers/staff, they attempted the epic failure of constructing "too much in one day." Thus their overall goal was diminished and the learning objectives lost. Additionally, the administration's credibility was lost as to future planning and trainings as the staff will associate all future trainings on this one event.

> **Pitfalls** All too often, training organizers try to incorporate too much information and knowledge into a single training and the learning objective becomes obscure and unmanageable. These coupled with poor execution (a result of planning) lead to professional development shortcomings.

Professional development for teachers can fall short in numerous ways, including:

- Too many (and sometimes conflicting) goals and priorities competing for teachers' time, energy, and attention.

> Having professional development too often lessens the effect of the trainings unless the concepts and theories are interwoven and are built as a continuum; thus sequential.

- Unrealistic expectations of how much time it will take schools and teachers to adopt and implement goals.

> Learning is a process and therefore must follow the same process and procedures for professional development implementation. It is unrealistic to think that the subject matters taught at a PD session will immediately be placed into practice and practiced routinely.

Administrators must note that their support, buy-in, and adoption of the contents taught and tenets will be instrumental in successful implementation and key when holding staff accountable.

- Professional development training events that are inappropriate in size, scope, or structure to support learning new ideas or skills.

> Gathering one hundred teachers into one room for a training event will never provide the time needed to reflect on the material, ask questions, listen to their peers, or engage in activities to enhance comprehension.

- Lack of support for teachers' implementation of new instructional practices.

> Research shows there's an implementation gap in teachers' professional development. They may learn, understand, and agree with a new idea or technique presented in a workshop, but find it hard for them to implement that idea without ongoing support.

The following are additional qualities of unrealistic expectations.

Instructional practices are oftentimes multidimensional and ill-communicated in terms of key priorities, takeaways, and implementation practices. This lack of communication aids in the breakdown of goal acquisition, this is a major pitfall. To combat this, administrators must "keep it simple." Therefore each year instructional properties (no more than three) must be identified in which the organization/school want teachers to learn, refine, or improve. Ideally, this selection should be in tandem with input from teachers themselves.

Ill-conceived notions that teachers will be able to implement and sustain professional development training themselves is rampant and is a myth that needs demystifying. It is my belief that introducing teachers to a new way to implement instructional content without the proper follow-up support only confuses and frustrates them. Be mindful that results will be forthcoming within the near future. This is a huge pitfall and one I address quite frequently. Just because a teacher attended training does not constitute immediate implementation. Teachers need time to absorb the information and techniques received as well as the resources and tools necessary to inquire as to additional implementation techniques and uses by their peers.

The establishment of vision is a school endeavor. The process and goal of education is one that belongs to the educational institution and therefore must be vetted and lead by the educational institutions themselves. This is a major PITFALL as establishing a concerted vision aids in the collaborative structures when bridging relations with administrators, organizers, facilitators, instructional teams, and community organizations.

This shift in processing facilitates the discovery of resources and shifts the role of accountability, rewards, and incentives, and ultimately the effectiveness of the system; thus professional development. In addition to the establishment of vision, resources when used effectively should include and involve the integration of community organizations.

Highly engaged educational institutions engage the whole community in establishing a common vision for student learning. Seek community leaders' ideas on major decisions about policies, changes in curriculum and instructional improvements, use of professional development resources, and budget.

Parents are definitely resources! If parents are not involved in the professional development of their schools' teachers, schools and districts alike are missing a valuable opportunity for engagement, continued support, and advocacy. For optimal support, engage parents and the larger community in ongoing dialogue about the changes needed to prepare more students for success in school, college, careers, and citizenship. Thus, educational institutions must work continually with parents and community leaders to ask and answer a variety of questions related to the common vision for school improvement, which includes professional development and engagement expectations.

Lastly, it is unrealistic to believe that professional development will be implemented optimally without administrators' and leaderships' active engagement and support. One method of support and engagement is that of "walkthroughs." One of the most important tools administrators and organizers can use to ensure instructional coherence and support is training in strategic classroom walkthroughs. Walkthroughs provide a critical link between assessment data and instructional practices.

Assessment data show who is succeeding and failing; strategic walkthroughs can help administrators (including teachers) learn why students are failing and how to turn failure into success. It is my philosophy that walkthroughs are to be supportive rather than punitive, and should be incorporated into capacity-building and succession-planning strategies by consistently involving personnel in the process, specifically asking for reflective thoughts and improvement recommendations.

Note that unrealistic expectations are not set in stone and can be overturned via education, commitment, and dedication to the process and audience; in this case professional development, student progress, and achievement results.

Reflective Notes

Are your professional development offerings unrealistic? How do you know you are focusing on the right topics (content)? How do you know you are meeting your team's needs?

1.
2.
3.
4.
5.
6.
7.

Additional notes for consideration:
_____
_____
_____
_____
_____
_____
_____
_____
_____

Professional development trainings must incorporate opportunities for reflections, processing, and connecting in order for transformations to take root.

Chapter 6

Empty Vessels

Teaching adults isn't like teaching children. Traditionally, children are viewed as empty vessels into which teachers can pour knowledge. Parents and teachers try to control the information that goes into the classroom to determine the quality of learning that comes out. Trainers cannot control adults this way. Children have little real-world experience upon which to base their learning. Adults have a great deal of accumulated experience that can enrich their education.

Adults can compare and contrast new knowledge against past learning. What we learn in childhood forms the foundation of what we learn as adults. Our life experiences can add to that, thus creating a substantial reservoir of information. Developing insight into how adults learn helps trainers become more successful.

Learning can be either passive or active. The traditional manner of education was by and large based on passive learning where the teacher is the expert and fount of all knowledge and the pupil is seen as the recipient of that expertise. The "mug and jug" theory was crafted in the late seventies and refers to an empty vessel (knowledge from the teacher—jugful of knowledge—which is given to the student to fill the deficit).

Today theorists of learning have recognized that simply giving attendees knowledge does not suggest or warrant the partaking of knowledge. The old saying "You can lead a horse to water but you can't make him drink" is paramount here. The attendee must have active involvement in the process, either mentally or physically or both, and a desire for knowledge for learning to occur. Returning to the horse metaphor, if the horse is thirsty it will drink; and if it drinks, its thirst will be quenched. The water alone cannot do the job.

Learners do not start as blank slates; information is not poured into an empty vessel. Rather, learners actively attempt to construct meaning; they are not passive bystanders. We need to know what learners know first before we can attempt to change it. The role of teaching is to understand learners' prior understanding and to guide them to other ways of thinking.

Learning is not rote regurgitation. Emphasis is on the individual. Yet, in many training programs for adults, the trainer decides on the content, and the principal training method is lecturing, occasionally accompanied by a demonstration. In these cases, the trainer/facilitator has the false sense of information as to their possessing the knowledge, and the participants, although adults, serving as empty vessels.

Pitfalls Freire recognized the inadequacy of this approach and called it banking of knowledge—storing up knowledge in the minds of learners for the future. It encourages learners to memorize facts and to learn information by rote measures. Unfortunately, this type of learning is short-lived as the learner retains very little of the information.

Implications for Teaching. Constructivism promotes using curricula customized to the students' prior knowledge. Hands-on problem solving is emphasized, and there is a focus on making connections between facts and fostering new understandings. Teachers rely heavily on open-ended questions and promote extensive dialogue among students. Assessment becomes part of the learning process so that students play a larger role in judging their own progress.

The job titles of the individuals who provide PD are many and varied—higher education faculty, trainers, program administrators in their training and technical assistance roles, individual consultants, child-care resources, referral training and technical assistance staff, and others deemed experts in the field. These professionals provide education, training, and/or technical asssitance to individuals working or preparing to work with students and their families and those working or preparing to work on behalf of children in training, licensing, resources, and other administrative roles related to education.

One huge pitfall within the professional development arena is that facilitators and expert presenters see themselves alone as the expert holding the entire body of knowledge within a given frame of reference, content, or subject matter. These presenters present with blinders on and see themselves as the one-and-only entity to relay information and convey meaning. The worst part of this syndrome is that most often administrators hand over control to presenters and leave them be stating, "Implement as needed; the training is yours to deliver."

During training sessions, participants should be encouraged to actively engage in the discovery of new meaning as well as the interpretation of old ideas and resources stemming from participants' experiences, expertise, and educational attainment. If participants are not allowed or encouraged to share this information, the basic tenets of how adults learn are forfeited and thus the learning environment becomes compromised; as adults will begin to retreat and consider the experts as sole warriors who disregard their contributions.

The empty-vessel syndrome is normally seen in the school

setting as teachers feel it's within their power to fill students' brains with their specific content knowledge. This is evident in the delivery format most teachers use as to lecture style and large-group activities. Yet those students who require a little more attention or direction are moved to the side as the learning objective and focus are centered on the masses rather than students' actual needs.

In the professional development setting, I don't feel as if facilitators will revert back to this mode of thinking. However, it is evident that many facilitators feel a body of specific expertise is theirs alone and thus own the sole body of knowledge versus that of encouraging the facilitation of a constructivist environment.

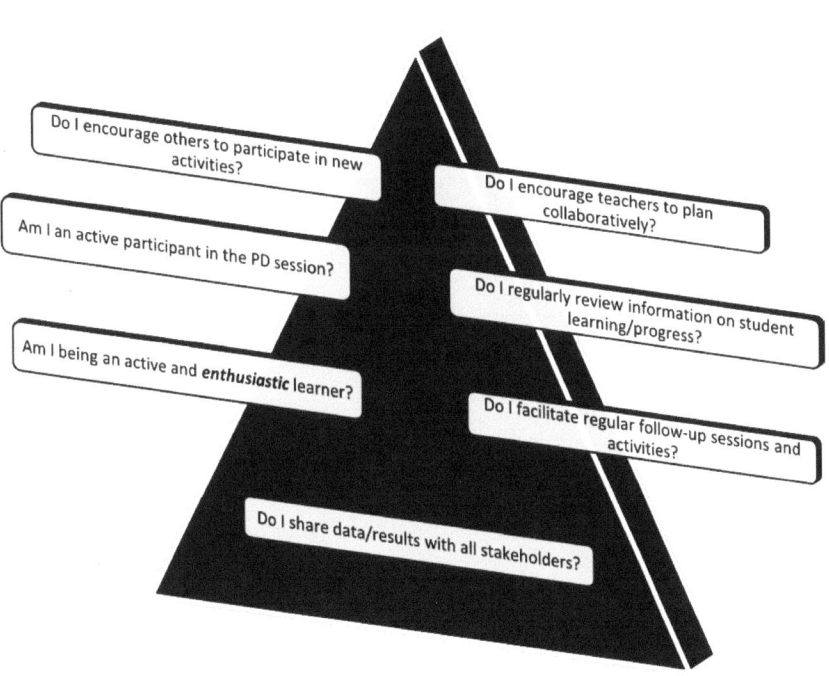

Facilitating learning in adults requires much more from the trainer than being simply a source of information. An effective trainer of adults will have to develop a training program and identify and use methods that meet the specific needs of the learners. It is essential that the trainer is capable of doing the following things:

- Absolutely master the content of the training (which is not always easy in a complex multidisciplinary field).

- Respond in a flexible way to specific questions/needs from the trainees.

- Handle the program in a creative and flexible way.

When professional development is approach using these tenets the training has a higher chance of being successful. The trainees feel respected, and are therefore more highly motivated. By adopting a participatory approach to the entire training process, through needs identification, planning, implementation, and evaluation, the trainer enters into partnership with the trainees as well as with other stakeholders. The learners become owners of the learning process, and the training program is adapted to their specific needs.

Reflective Notes

Learning can be either passive or active. Explain the steps you will embrace to move your professional development opportunities from a passive engagement to an active engagement.

1.
2.
3.
4.
5.
6.
7.

Additional notes for consideration:
_____
_____
_____
_____
_____
_____
_____
_____
_____
_____
_____
_____

The greatest areas of struggle are not in learning a new skill but in implementing it!

CHAPTER 7

Implementation Dip

Whenever you try to implement something new, there is going to be a period of adjustment. Scores will go down if we are talking tests, classroom behaviors will change, and achievement will go down if new teaching strategies are being implemented. In short, any time you try something new, it is NOT going to go exactly as planned! Mistakes will happen, things will be bad before they get better—it's part of the whole change process. Which is why we need to be implementing changes slowly, early, and over time, so things that go wrong can be adjusted.

What is the implementation dip? Fullan defines the "implementation dip" as "the inevitable bumpiness and difficulties encountered as people learn new behaviors and beliefs." In *Leading in a Culture of Change* (2001), Fullan writes, "the implementation dip is literally a dip in performance and confidence as one encounters an innovation that requires new skills and new understandings. All innovations worth their salt call upon people to question and in some respects to change their behavior and their beliefs—even in cases where innovations are pursued voluntarily." What happens when you find yourself needing new skills and are not being proficient when you are used to knowing what you are doing? How do you feel when you are called upon to do something new and are not clear about what to do and do not understand the knowledge and value base of new belief systems?

In all forms of learning a new skill, mere knowledge of it is never as difficult as its implementation. Think about this in the context of sports. If a football coach wants to improve his team, he might begin by working on the fundamentals of blocking. In other words, he recognizes

20 THE NUMBER ON AVERAGE OF SEPARATE INSTANCES OF PRACTICE IT TAKES A TEACHER TO MASTER A NEW SKILL, THIS NUMBER INCREASES WITH **SKILL COMPLEXITITY** (GULAMAHUSSEIN, 2013).

the player's lack of knowledge of a particular strategy, in this case blocking, will improve their results. He might explain the concepts of closing, demonstrate the skill (modeling), and even have players practice blocking during practice. However, when players initially begin to implement the new skill on the field it does not transfer smoothly, as players are used to playing the game in their old form and fashion (without the blocking techniques). Thus the other parts of their performance have to change to compensate for the new-found skills. Hence, the greatest areas of struggle are not in learning a new skill but in implementing it (Gulamhussein, 2015).

The implementation dip is true with a new skill—learning how to cut a pineapple isn't as difficult as actually cutting the pineapple or learning the fundamentals of riding a bike isn't as difficult as actually riding a bike. In most cases, research has documented that one's first attempt at any new skill fails. Various reasons are cited, from those being the implementer's unfamiliarity with the basic elements, stress, the shear disappointment of failing, or one's inability to feel confident and let his/her team or in this case students down. The implementation dip is further complicated by the fact that researchers show teachers change their underlying beliefs about how to teach a concept only after they personally acknowledge success.

Administrators, this is an area where your professionalism, demeanor, and confidence in your teaching team should be exerted; as your team should have the opportunity to practice the newly taught skill multiple times prior to being held accountable for its implementation, thus noticeable change. Encourage teachers to try the newly acquired information/strategies with support of other team members also attending the training. And better yet, explain to their students, if appropriate, that you will be trying a new implementation strategy. This is also a great area to employ coaching techniques and learning communities' discussions as not all teachers will experience the implementation dip, and strategies of successful implementation can prevent stress for others.

Effective professional development should incorporate practical application offerings as a component to distill some of these stressors and hopefully dismantle the dip. Yet, I stand aware the environment changes as soon as one reenters their classroom and faces his/her students.

Teachers are giving up after the unsuccessful implementation of the newly acquire skill. Thus they feel inadequate to implement, which equates back to the training being null and void. To offset this dip, administrators, coaches, and support teams alike must stand willing and ready to support, reteach, and model skills during the implementation phase of the concepts learned.

A glitch with the implementation dip seems to be that teachers only internalize and change their beliefs when they see success with their students. But student success is hard to achieve initially, since new skills and teaching strategies take time to master. Therefore, administrators must be armed at the outset and prepared to support the change process.

As more and more researchers and educators realize traditional staff development workshops have not provided the type of ongoing, meaningful learning opportunities teachers need to grow professionally, literature has increased the emphasis on the critical role of sustained, ongoing, professional development connected to everyday experiences at a level commensurate with teacher ability and skill level.

Harwell (2003) found that sustained, ongoing, intensive professional development is more likely to impact instructional practice on a broader level than are shorter, limited-staff development workshops. However, one major problem exists: Many schools are not organized or structured in such a way to promote ongoing, meaningful, professional development connected to everyday classroom experiences. Therefore, schools need to shift the focus towards organizational structures that promote the type of continual learning necessary to enhance teacher expertise (Farrell & Little, 2005).

So how do leaders prepare for, deal with, and overcome the implementation dip?

1. Create awareness – Let teacher teams know that an implementation dip is inevitable. Change theory tells us we will experience it if we are truly engaging in meaningful change and cultural shifts. Make it a discussion at staff meetings or during team collaborative times. Knowing that we will dip and then talking about how to deal with it can build the resiliency needed to continue forward with the work.

2. Pause to reflect – When the dip hits and staff are feeling overwhelmed, use it as a time to pause and reflect. Identify celebrations that have come as a result of the work. Reflect upon what has been accomplished, taking stock of the great work done thus far. Ask what further refinements could be done to the frameworks and processes. Basically, take some time to reflect and

regroup. Letting teams know it's okay to take a break to recharge can also function to further build trust for the leader, recognizing and responding to the needs of the staff rather than "powering through it."

3. Support – As leaders, this is the time we also need to take an active role within teams, saying, "What can I do to help?" and rolling up the sleeves to go through the mud with your teams. Whether joining teams for meetings, providing additional resources, or being that perennial cheerleader, school leaders play a crucial role when teams encounter the implementation dip. Without recognition and support, teams can either 1) give up, or 2) see giving up as not an option and foster resentment for the leaders in continuing to pursue the initiative. Support for teams is never more critical than during this phase.

 The good news is that by preparing and responding proactively to the implementation dip, leaders can ensure the bumps teams encounter are not impassable barriers. It is the normal part of the learning process we expect students to engage in and natural in the evolution of a collaborative culture within a school. Engaging the dip with eyes open and responses prepared can ensure it doesn't mean the end for engaging in collaborative frameworks.

 Sustaining a yearly professional learning can be a challenge. Maintaining energy and commitment for continued learning requires not only focus and determination, but also a substantial enough goal to drive a school/organizational focus all year. A school culture that values continuous professional development can sustain innovations in teaching and increase the likelihood that those innovations will result in achievement for students. Strategies to share and sustain improvement, nurture knowledge gained, and new practices learned should be built into the original plan for professional learning.

Peaks & Pitfalls

"We've considered every potential risk except the risks of avoiding all risks."

Reflective Notes

How do I motivate teachers to begin implementing new knowledge, skills, or strategies? How can I plan to strategically support teachers through an "implementation dip?"

1.
2.
3.
4.
5.
6.
7.

Additional notes as to the implementation dip:

_____
_____
_____
_____
_____
_____
_____
_____
_____
_____

Appendices

Appendix A

Examples of Sample Schedules

1. Half-Day Workshops

2. Full-Day Workshops

3. Half-Day Workshops

4. Multi-Day Workshops

5. Multiple Presenters

6. Sequential Workshops (Learning Communities)

Schedule for Half-Day Workshops
(Less Than Fifty Attendees)

Best Practices Tip:
As you begin to plan and prepare for the day, please keep the following in mind as you organize and outline your day. Remember this is just a sample; however, it is derived from best practices—modify as needed.

Session Topic: Provide the name of the training, including clarifiers as needed.

Length of Training: 4.0 hours of instruction, including three breaks (ensure you include at least one hands-on or group activity each hour).

Key Concepts: What are the key concepts you will introduce? These should be aligned with your goals and objectives.

Key Objectives: What are your objectives? For a half-day workshop, you should identify two to three objectives that your participants will master (one each hour).

Objective 1: Objective 2/3:

Implementation Procedures: Define the flow of the day. Identify group and experiential activities versus that of self-reflection and presenter facilitation. This is your actual agenda/schedule for the day. Be creative in your approach as to design with your participants' learning styles in mind.

Activities and Timeline:

15 minutes – Introductions and agenda review, informing participants about the day's purpose. Includes opportunities for pre-assessment if not completed prior to arrival.

45 minutes – Facilitator-led discussions, group work, and objective review

Break – 15 minutes

10 minutes – Connecting activity (designed to reconvene the group and to increase participant participation and connections). This could be via the incorporation of music and movement, self-discovery then sharing, or via mnemonic exercises.

30 minutes – Facilitator-led discussions/activities

20 minutes – Experiential learning opportunities and reflection

Break – 10 minutes

5 minutes – Connecting activity

20 minutes – Group work and objective demonstration

20 minutes – Facilitator-led discussions and connection to objectives and activities

15 minutes – Participant reflection. Most often this is performed at the end of the session. However, to ensure understanding by participants, this is a great opportunity to address questions or clarify learning objectives by participants. Facilitators should optimize on this by documenting questions, thoughts, and comments, and reviewing these then or at the end of the session.

Break – 10 minutes

10 minutes – Group work. During this time, facilitator decides how to address questions or comments.

10 minutes – Facilitator-led activity and discussions

10 minutes – Q&A, evaluations, closing thoughts from facilitators and organizers

Schedule for Full-Day Workshops
(Less Than Fifty Attendees)

Best Practices Tip:
As you begin to plan and prepare for the day, please keep the following in mind as you organize and outline your day. Remember this is just a sample. However, it is derived from best practices. Modify as needed.

Session Topic: Provide the name of the training, including clarifiers as needed.

Length of Training: 8.0 hours of instruction, including five breaks (ensure you include at least two hands-on or group activities each hour).

Key Concepts: What are the key concepts you will introduce? These should be aligned with your goals and objectives. For an eight-hour training, I would incorporate at least two key concepts. Concepts are in line with goals and thus different from your objectives as stated below.

Key Objectives: What are you objectives? For a full-day workshop, you should identify three to four objectives that your participants will master.

Objective 1: Objective 2: Objective 3/4:

Implementation Procedures: Define the flow of the day. Identify group and experiential activities versus that of self-reflection and presenter facilitation. This is your actual agenda/schedule for the day. Be creative in your approach as to design with your participants' learning styles in mind.

Activities and Timeline:

25 minutes – Introductions and agenda review, discussion as to purpose, goal, and objectives.

15 minutes – Conduction of and review of pre-assessment.

20 minutes – Facilitator-led discussions

Break – 15 minutes

15 minutes – Connecting activity (designed to reconvene the group and to increase participant participation and connections). This could be via the incorporation of music and movement, self-discovery then sharing, or via mnemonic exercises.

15 minutes – Group work and objective review (objective review—to ensure participants understand the learning objectives)

30 minutes – Facilitator-led discussions/activities—includes multiple modes of delivery

20 minutes – Experiential learning opportunities and reflection

Break – 15 minutes

10 minutes – Connecting activity (the ability to connect with your participants and allow opportunities for them to connect and interact. Emphasizes the need for a promotion of professional learning communities and peer-to-peer learning and support). This is not a frivolous activity but is grounded in research and best practices as one that adds dimensions to a workshop/training. This is similar to networking but is completed throughout the day via directed connections and individual explorations.

20 minutes – Group work and objective demonstration

Lunch – 1 hour (Thirty minutes of this should be free time—allows for reflection, continued group discussions, or time to refocus as needed). This time is equally important for the presenter as he/she also needs time to regroup and reflect as well as prepare/adjust for the afternoon session.

30 minutes – Facilitator-led discussions and connection to objectives and activities

15 minutes – Participant reflection. Most often this is performed at the end of the session. However, to ensure understanding by participants, this is a great opportunity to address questions or clarify learning objectives by participants. Facilitators should optimize on this by documenting questions, thoughts, and comments, and reviewing these then or at the end of the session.

Break – 10 minutes

30 minutes – Group work. During this time, before facilitator decides how to address questions or comments.

30 minutes – Facilitator-led activity and discussions. Notice the length of time of afternoon facilitator discussions. These are lessened as to the attention span after lunch and in the afternoon. These facilitated sessions should highlight specific and pertinent information in short spurts followed by a hands-on activity or group work.

Break – 10 minutes

30 minutes – Group presentation and discussions

25 minutes – Facilitator-led discussion and/or wrap-ups

Break – 10 minutes

15 minutes – Q&A. Facilitator should ask questions if attendees do not pose these. Review of parking lots

10 minutes – Closing thoughts from facilitators and organizers

5 minutes – Evaluations

Schedule for Multi-Day Workshops
(2.5 Days)

Workshop Summary:
Include in this section a summary of the workshop goals and objectives to be accomplished as well as the rationale for the selection of these and a timeline (2 days or 2.5 days). This is also a great place to outline the days as to experiential activities, group work, and facilitator discussions (single vs. multiple). Lastly, outline here the committee desires as to how this information will be used to determine return on investment to either students, districts, organizations, or communities.

Day 1:

25 minutes – Introduction, review of goals, format, facilitation, etc.

10 minutes – Connecting activity

35 minutes – Facilitator-led discussion

Break – 15 minutes

15 minutes – Connecting activity

45 minutes – Facilitator-led discussion

15 minutes – Group activity

Break – **15** minutes

1.5 hours – Group assignment and charge led by facilitator

Lunch – 1 hour

2.5 hours – Group work

1 hour – Facilitator-led discussion and items to consider for group. This is completed via small-group roundtables.

20 minutes – Wrap-up for the day and reflections

Day 2:
The next day, participants will embark on a variety of group and hands-on activities designed to intertwine the learning concepts from Day 1. The later part of the day will center on group sharing and exploration as to innovative concepts, techniques, and tips. Lastly, Day 2 will end with self-reflection as to the integration of concepts within their respective educational establishments.

20 minutes – Welcome, goal/mission review, and discussion as to the day's events and activities.

10 minutes – Connection activity

2 hours – Group work and rotations

Break – 15 minutes

1.5 hours – Group work and rotations

Break – 15 minutes

40 minutes – Group report-outs – led by facilitator

25 minutes – Facilitator bridge and engagement discussions as to previous activities and next steps

Lunch – 1 hour (remember to allow at least thirty minutes for personal care time and/or quite reflection)

10 minutes – Connecting activities

45 minutes – Facilitator-led discussions and activities

15 minutes – Mnemonic activities and other experimental activities to bridge learning

20 minutes – Facilitator-led wrap-up and charge for next day

Day 3:

10 minutes – Connections

15 minutes – Reflections and charge for today

30 minute – Facilitator-led activities, discussion as to breakout activities

2 hours – Theory into practice – This is core to a multi-day workshops. How does a teacher take a concept from theory into practice? Participants should use this time to outline their timeline and strategy for successful communication with administrators and in developing a plan of action. This work should be completed via individual work but can be performed in tandem with professional learning communities especially if teachers from the same school are present. During this time, the facilitator is there for support, questions, and to provide assistance as necessary.

Break – 10 minutes

45 minutes – Facilitator-led activity and wrap-up

15 minutes – Q&A

15 minutes – Evaluations

Schedule for Workshops with Multiple Presenters

This particular schedule is a one-day schedule with four presenters/facilitators. This is a typical configuration for early education centers; thus my rationale for including it in this book and for redesigning a best practices version.

20 minutes – Overview and flow of day, introduction as to presenters, and subject, goals, and objectives

10 minutes – Connecting activity

40 minutes – Facilitator-led discussion and activity; integrating opportunity for group work.

Break – 15 minutes

1.5 hours – Speaker rotation. Participants will be divided into several groups and asked to sit at a roundtable. Speakers will travel from table to table for small-group discussions and activities designed to enhance the learning objectives.

Break – 15 minutes

1 hour – Group rotation continues. Groups should be comprised of ten or less participants. A typical discussion would last thirty minutes, which would include question-and-answer opportunities.

Lunch – 1 hour (allow thirty minutes for personal reflection and needs time)

15 minutes – Connection activity

45 minutes – Interactive keynote address

Break – 15 minutes

45 minutes – Facilitator-led experiential activity

15 minutes – Reflection opportunity – journaling and small group

Break – 10 minutes

20 minutes – Q&A

10 minutes – Evaluations and adjournment

Schedule for Sequential Workshops
(Such as Those Connected to Learning Communities)

20 Minutes – Connecting activity

20 minutes – Introduction and review of past/current goals and objectives

20 minutes – Review of homework; review of roles and expectations (as needed); review agenda for the day. Determine if everyone is on track or if modifications/issues need addressing.

20 minutes – Discussion of assigned readings (all responsible), sharing, and reflecting on classroom experiences and reviewing student work

Break – 15 minutes

15 minutes – Introduction of new topic/format for discovery and delivery

45 minutes – Facilitator-led discussion/presentation (multidimensional)

15 minutes – Q&A

Break – 15 minutes

40 minutes – Facilitator-led discussion and activities

Lunch – 1 hour (allowing time for silent reflection)

2.5 hours – Learning community group work linked to objectives and students goals/outcomes (facilitator to support via traveling stations, incorporation of lending libraries, and other support structures)

40 minutes – Group report-outs and discussions

20 minutes – Wrap-up and goal setting for next session

15 minutes – Evaluations

APPENDIX B

Implementation Items to Ponder When Crafting Optimal-Learning Goals and Objectives

1. As student data is reviewed, how does this impede upon professional development goals/objectives?

2. Are proposed training topics specifically aligned with the goals of the organization/district? Are these aligned to student outcomes?

3. Who is our target audience? Educators yes, but what level of educator and/or professional? Remember that your training should be tailored to your audience, so this questions should weigh heavily on your learning goals and objectives.

4. Budgetary constraints – How much has been allocated to support this training? Are there sufficient funds to cover all related expenses (e.g., location, presenters, materials, etc.)?

5. Does your training align with current or existing trainings? If so, how? Will this training be viewed as a duplication?

6. What processes will you use to identify, discuss, and implement learning goals and objectives?

7. What will administrators use to determine success? Is teacher success connected? Student driven? Or a combination of both?

Learning goals is an easily identified action that a participant is expected to demonstrate in terms of knowledge, skills, and abilities upon the completion of a training. When crafting learning goals, the following is an easy template to follow:

- Focus on the end result of your training.

- What measurement tool will you employ to ensure the learning objective is met?

- Use simple, specific action verbs to describe what participants are expected to demonstrate upon completion of the training.

APPENDIX C
Evaluation Forms

1. Transformative Evaluation
2. Reflective Evaluation
3. Optimal Evaluation
4. Succinct and Direct Evaluation
5. Interactive Evaluation
6. Before, During, and After Evaluation
7. Seven-Question Evaluation

SAMPLE EVALUATION FORMS

According to both Guskey (1998) and Kirkpatrick (2006), it is exceedingly difficult to prove the impact of professional development. To do so, one would need to control all other factors that may influence the results. While both authors suggest applying an experimental evaluation design when possible (i.e., comparing results of experimental vs. control groups), both concede this approach is often impractical to implement.

In the absence of proof, the value of professional development evaluation is measured by the quality of evidence it provides. This evidence can be used by training providers toward improving their current trainings and designing new offerings. As consumers of professional development, it can also be used by local program administrators, teachers, and staff to inform their selection of offerings. Therefore, the goal of the proposed evaluation framework is to collect the strongest possible evidence regarding the effectiveness of professional development in terms of satisfaction, learning, behavior, and impact. The following evaluative tools were conceived with the intentions to gather the most accurate and reliable information to inform future professional development offerings.

1. Transformative Evaluation
2. Reflective Evaluation
3. Optimal Evaluation
4. Succinct and Direct Evaluation
5. Interactive Evaluation
6. Before, During, and After Evaluation
7. Seven-Question Evaluation

Transformative Sample Evaluation

This type of evaluation captures one's ability to transform their practices and current frames of reference to include newly introduced theories and those associated with best practices. I believe these evaluations should consist of narratives as one's opinions and thoughts are most reflective when received in written form versus those collected primarily by bubbles and circulation.

1. The learning objectives of the training were?

2. These goals will be implemented into my classroom via the following courses of action.

3. To fully implement these goals and objectives, the following is needed from:
    Administrators/Organization?
    Students?
    Myself?
    Budgetary perspectives?

4. The impact of this newly acquired knowledge will be apparent when?

5. Overall the training met my needs in the following manner:

6. If I could change any aspect of the training this would be reflected by:

7. The environment of the training was conductive and fostered opportunities for growth and professional exchange.

8. The material and resources were adequate and if not was readily made available.

9. Elaborate on additional training needs needed to fully implement the presented goals/objectives.

10. The presenter/facilitator was knowledgeable, however could have been more effective if?

11. I will be able to effectively affect change within my organizational structure and culture based on the learning I have obtained during this session.

Sample Reflective Evaluation

My goal for attending the workshop/training was:

The workshop/training goal was to _____

Was the goal accomplished? Y/N   Why or Why Not? _____

List three things from your session that you learned today and discuss how you will implement these into your classroom structure two weeks from now.

1.

2.

3.

Using the scale, rate your thoughts on the following (5 – fantastic, 4 – good, 3 – average, 2 – basic, 1 – below average):

Environment:

Room décor

Room comfortability

Microphones/technology

Content:
Was the presenter knowledgeable?

Did this knowledge articulate to best practices and research in which you can relate and employ?

Was the information clearly understandable and relatable?

Process:
How would you rate the manner in which the presentation and agenda flowed?

Did opportunities allow for engagement/participation? Y/N

Was this helpful in the acquisition of new knowledge?

I will remember the following from the training:

This training has supplied me with enough tools/techniques and knowledge to engage others on the topic and effectively discuss organizational structure and culture with my director/administrators.

I would like additional information as to:

I have the following questions:

Optimal Sample Evaluation

Session

1. The topic presented was well represented by the workshop description.
   (strongly disagree) (disagree) (neutral) (agree) (strongly agree)

2. The topic presented was easy to understand/comprehend.
   (strongly disagree) (disagree) (neutral) (agree) (strongly agree)

3. The materials for the workshop were well prepared.
   (strongly disagree) (disagree) (neutral) (agree) (strongly agree)

4. The length of the workshop was adequate for the topic covered.
   (strongly disagree) (disagree) (neutral) (agree) (strongly agree)

Presenter

5. The presenter was well prepared for the workshop.
   (strongly disagree) (disagree) (neutral) (agree) (strongly agree)

6. The presenter used examples that made the topic easier to understand.
   (strongly disagree) (disagree) (neutral) (agree) (strongly agree)

7. The presenter took time to answer my question(s) and foster understanding.
   (strongly disagree) (disagree) (neutral) (agree) (strongly agree)

Participant Information

8. I plan to integrate the skills gained in this workshop into my daily structure.
   (strongly disagree) (disagree) (neutral) (agree) (strongly agree)

9. I feel comfortable learning new concepts and in applying best practices.
(strongly disagree) (disagree) (neutral) (agree) (strongly agree)

10. I feel the information presented enables me to support my center's culture, goals, and objectives via the acquisition of new knowledge that is relevant and pertinent to my position.
(strongly disagree) (disagree) (neutral) (agree) (strongly agree)

Please use the space below to provide additional feedback

_____
_____
_____
_____
_____

Succinct and Direct Sample Evaluation

This example of professional development evaluation is short, concise, and to the point as to the items it measures as well as summation of data. These evaluations are key when accessing the same teachers over a course of time as well as those with limited speaking or language acquisition skills.

Training Topic: _____ Date: _____

Please rate the following:

Overall Training:

	Strongly Agree	Agree	Neutral	Disagree	Strongly Disagree
I am satisfied with today's training.					
Handouts were engaging and useful in following the presenter.					
Workshop time allowed for practical implication of skills and best practices discussed.					
The atmosphere was enthusiastic, interesting, and conducive to professional exchange.					
Session content and strategies are applicable to my work.					

What was the major idea or concept taught today?

_____

_____

How will you incorporate these concepts/ideas in your learning structure? _____

_____

Workshop Presenter: (please circle your response)

The presenter aligned the objectives of the training with your professional development needs.

      Strongly Agree   Agree   Neutral   Disagree   Strongly Disagree

The presenter presented strong in his/her knowledge of the subject matter and was able to articulate such knowledge.

      Strongly Agree   Agree   Neutral   Disagree   Strongly Disagree

The presenter was able to relate to me as a professional and aided in the creation of a supportive environment.

      Strongly Agree   Agree   Neutral   Disagree   Strongly Disagree

I am pleased with the training attended today and look forward to additional training opportunities.

      Strongly Agree   Agree   Neutral   Disagree   Strongly Disagree

INTERACTIVE SAMPLE EVALUATION

The interactive sample evaluation is a tool I devised three years ago as I began to consistently facilitate professional development trainings. As the subject matter expert on the topics I facilitated, I wanted to be able to address participants' questions and gauge understanding during and after my trainings. Thus I wanted a tool that supported such information and detail. Evaluations are often given to training organizers who are left to address content-specific questions and to inquire as to growth, yet many are unsure of the next steps in terms of meeting the participants' needs if the objective was not obtained.

As a facilitator, I collaborated with organizers to measure and support participants' growth as well as to identify areas where additional support and training was needed to master the concept and foster understanding. Note that this evaluation was submitted to the organizers with copies given to me of those needing feedback/follow-up. My follow-up was manifested in the form of e-mail communication to both the organizer and participant for monitoring purposes.

Training attended: _____ Location: _____
Date of Training: _____

Impact on Professional Practices:

This training enhanced the participant's content knowledge and facilitated methods of growth and implementation.
Yes   No
Please explain your answer: _____
_____
_____

The training enabled me to visualize the discussed concepts/best practices and to think strategically as to implementation.
Yes   No
Please explain your answer: _____
_____
_____
_____

The training enhanced the participant's professional growth and deepened your reflection and self-assessment of exemplary practices.
Yes   No
Please explain your answer: _____
_____
_____
_____

The goals and objectives taught today were integral to my daily activities and classroom environment.
Yes   No
Please explain your answer: _____
_____
_____
_____
_____

Please rate the following
(5 being superior and 1 being inadequate)

	5	4	3	2	1
The training was well organized and met my needs as a participant.					
The training goals and objectives were clearly explained and met.					
The environment was supportive and fostered a warm and nurturing setting for professional exchange and learning.					
All necessary materials/resources/equipment were provided or made readily available.					
Facilitator presented as an expert and appeared knowledgeable as to the content area and best practices.					
Hands-on and group discussions aided in the facilitation of knowledge acquisition and increased my understanding of the content taught.					

The goal of professional development is to enhance one's understanding of the training concepts/goals and provide tools to aid in best-practices implementation and goal acquisition. Do you feel this goal was achieved during this training? Were there barriers to goal acquisition? Please provide additional thoughts and comments as to the training in terms of effectiveness, needs and overall satisfaction.

_____
_____
_____
_____
_____
_____
_____
_____

If you would like further discussion or contact as to this training, please indicate this here and provide your contact information:

_____
_____
_____
_____
_____
_____
_____
_____
_____
_____

Name:

Contact Information (E-mail):

Organization:

Before, During, and After Sample Evaluation

An alternative approach to capturing satisfaction data at the end of a session is to build in specific points for checking in with participants throughout a professional development event. The sample questions are arranged to show the progression from the start of the session to the end.

Before questions can be noted on flip charts located around the room as well as forms passed out in various phases (before, during, and after product). During questions can be collected at the lunch break via small-group discussion, a chart walk, or by another short form that is easily collected. If the session or PD offering is held through Web-based technology chat sessions are perfect manners to collect ongoing evaluations, thoughts, and comments. The after evaluation forms can be collected in the same fashions as chart walks and group discussions but can also be obtained by question and answers with facilitators and organizers.

BEFORE	DURING	AFTER
What are your goals for attending this session?	Is this session allowing you to meet your goals?	Were your goals for attending this session met?
List the goals of this session.	Is the session meeting the listed goals?	Did the session meet the listed goals?
What are your expectations for this training?	Is the training meeting your expectations?	Was the training what you expected?
What content are you hoping to gain based upon presented goals and referenced material?	Is the content as presented relatable and understood?	Was the content presented in a manner to engage your thoughts as to best practices and implementation methods?
The environment/staff seems warm, inviting, and nurturing and fosters learning.	The environment/staff is supportive, conductive, and nurturing.	The environment/staff yields itself to a quality learning environment/experience.

Seven-Question Evaluation

Ideal for Usage with Professional Learning Communities Sessions

This evaluation is designed specifically to evaluate the professional development and goals associated with professional learning communities. Questions posed here are those built upon a continuum fostering growth and implementation over a period of time.

Questions for Guiding Thoughts:

1. Was time allowed for the introduction and practicing of new concepts/theories?

2. Was the atmosphere enthusiastic, interesting, and conductive to a collegial professional exchange as demonstrated?

3. Were the goals and objectives of the training clear and in alignment with those introduced via the professional learning community and prior trainings?

4. Did I learn useful strategies and implementation methods to enhance classroom instruction?

5. Did this session allow me the opportunity to foster growth in my colleagues, my students, and myself? Provide examples.

6. Am I able to effect change within my school's culture or organizational structure with the knowledge I have obtained? Do I feel secure in my knowledge to advocate for this change? If not, do I need additional skills in the following areas to effect change and advocate as to organizational structure/culture?

7. Was the facilitator open to discussions, shared best practices, and supportive of the learning goals while addressing and fostering a warm, inviting, and nurturing learning environment?

Note that I did not place lines after each question as I wanted to create opportunities of personal reflection and comments that I may not have disclosed. Ideally, these questions are used as guiding thoughts to incite conversations and begin the thinking phase.

APPENDIX D
Sample Note-Taking Form
Four "As" Protocol

Assumptions: What assumptions does the presenter foster?	**Agreements:** From the items presented, what do you hold true and agree with?
Arguments: Where do you disagree with the items presented/facilitator?	**Aspirations:** From the items presented, what do you aspire to achieve?

APPENDIX E
Professional Development Quotes

"Professional development is most effective when it addresses the concrete, everyday challenges involved in teaching and learning of specific academic subject matters." (National Staff Development Council, 2009)

"Everyone thinks of changing the world; but no one thinks of changing himself. Professional development begins with oneself and then penetrates one's students/organization/environment." (Fullan, 2000)

"While the ultimate goal of teacher professional development is to improve student's learning, the more immediate goal is to improve teacher knowledge, skills, and practice." (Gulamhussein, 2014)

"Involving teachers in data collection and later in data analysis will almost certainly extend and enrich their professional learning. In addition, involving teachers in evaluating their professional development is worthwhile because it establishes their ownership of the effort as well as the results." (Miller, 1995)

"Because professional development is a shared responsibility, it is important to engage as many people as possible in conversations about professional development and their roles in the process." (Zarrow, 2014)

"Leadership is key to establishing school cultures that encourage and support professional learning." (Nagel, 2013)

"One cannot enhance teachers' knowledge and skill without also addressing what teachers know about reaching individual students and the actual curriculum that teachers are expected to teach." (Haslam, 2008)

Appendix F
Innovative Approaches to Sustain Professional Development Offerings

1. Develop partnerships with community and philanthropic agencies. This partnership not only can provide organizational structures and partner agency benefits but can also provide funding streams, a wider impact as to service areas, and in the collective of bridging gaps and reducing duplication of services or one-offs implementation issues.

2. Properly evaluate and analysis training development components. I would recommend a 360-degree evaluation.

3. Maintain a culture of ongoing learning by fostering a mixture of professional development approaches. For example, an optimal professional development series or offerings should include traditional avenues such as conferences, college courses (CEUs), and district workshops, in addition to fostering collaboration via the building of professional learning communities and internal communications.

4. Professional development is embedded into participants' weekly structure and is considered key as to their duties, roles, and responsibilities. Thus it is job embedded and becomes a component of the participants' personnel evaluation, therefore accountable. This ability allows for complete implementation of content and best practices.

5. Integrate a de-stressor prior to the beginning of the training session. This process engages the brain (provides oxygen), clears thoughts, and prepares the mind for engagement and the learning of new skills and concepts. I introduce these de-stressors as connectors or connecting activities. In my mind, these are similar to greeting my students each morning through breathing and stretching activities.

6. Obtain participants' feedback and when possible their thoughts on design, presenters, and experiential activities on which to employ. Participants should have as much buy-in as possible, equating to full partnerships and activities promotion.

7. Implement webinars into your professional development offerings. Best practices are that webinars should complement previous sessions and serve as a follow-up to speaker-based series. Webinars should be practical, thought provoking, and formulated with intent, goals, and objectives in mind.

Testimonies

Dr. Hall understands the importance of providing a rich and rigorous training environment for all staff. She is aware that it must be both challenging and rewarding—offering a combination of lecture, hands-on activities, and time for networking among attendees. Our staff at The King's Daughter's Child Development Center have benefited greatly from the training opportunities facilitated by Dr. Hall.

Candyee Goode, *Executive Director*
King's Daughters Child Development Center
Madison, Tennessee

Dr. Rena Hall continues to amaze me with her ability to design, facilitate, and implement quality and innovative professional development trainings. As the director of Pre-K for a large urban public school system, I have witnessed Dr. Hall collaborate with district office administrators, individual school, and community sites to identify specific needs in order to design the appropriate trainings that are unique to each site and the public school system's goals.

When Dr. Hall began working with the district she found that educators were at varying levels of understanding and abilities to implement instruction. I was immediately impressed with her professionalism, candor, and ability to relate to others as she began her work to evaluate and provide the appropriate professional development framework needed. After participating in-group training sessions or one-on-one trainings, teachers and administrators have commented on Dr. Hall's knowledge of the subject matter and her ability to deliver and share information in a way that is understandable and non-intimidating.

Dr. Hall understands the importance of ongoing trainings that are design to scaffold the learning to meet the end goals and outcomes desired. She makes herself available to provide follow-up and clarification to all participants. Teachers, educational assistants, families, and administrators who have participated in trainings provided by Dr. Hall have been enriched with the knowledge and confidence needed to effectively implement instruction and programming for success.

Phyllis Phillips
Director of Pre-Kindergarten Programs
Metropolitan Nashville Public Schools
Nashville, Tennessee

Dr. Hall is a respected and credible name in education. She has provided innovative and high-quality learning opportunities to many educators. She understands it is vital to school success and teacher satisfaction. Dr. Hall does a wonderful job of taking research and illuminating how teachers make a visible difference in children's learning. Creating lifelong learners is her goal. Her behavior is extremely professional, which also reflects in her positive attitude as a natural leader. She leads by inspiration and instills a sense of confidence in her team members.

Nancy McClellan
Literacy Coach
Nashville, Tennessee

Dr. Rena Hall consistently exceeds my expectations for effective trainings in professional learning. Serving a national customer base, she has the ability to design and facilitate customized trainings to best meet the needs of each audience. Dr. Hall's extensive experience in both the classroom and as a leader of professional development supports her ability to relate to others. Participants comment on her ability to meet them where they are and offer new and innovative strategies based on experience. As a consultant colleague, I respect her candor, professionalism, and ability to create a cohesive training environment.

Dianne Patterson
Professional Learning
Frog Street Press
Grapevine, Texas

I am very pleased with the exceptional professional development training Dr. Rena Hall provided to my staff. Her professionalism throughout the entire process and her honesty and ability to relate to others are what made the difference.

Dr. Rena listened to our needs and designed and developed quality professional training that met those needs. The trainings were well prepared with research-based materials. During her presentation she created a warm and open learning environment that captured the attention of my staff. Dr. Rena has that rare ability of engaging an audience and creating an environment for learning through the use of hands-on experiences and thought-provoking materials. The staff could relate and identify with her training and left the sessions excited about the chance to use the techniques, information, and materials.

Dr. Rena's training has helped our staff improve their professionalism and classroom management, as well as given them the ability to build positive relationships with children and their parents. We have experienced a 50-percent increase in parent involvement, less behavior issues due to better classroom management, and the teachers are doing more intentional teaching in the classrooms. In addition, the culture of the center is changing due to the confidence the staff developed as a result of the training given by Dr. Rena.

I highly recommend Dr. Rena Hall to anyone in need of professional development trainings.

Mahalia Howard
Executive Director
Grace M. Eaton Child Care & Early Learning Center
Nashville, Tennessee

Napier Enhanced Option School recently transformed its pre-K program from decent to exceptional through a partnership with United Way of Nashville. Without the leadership, direction, and guidance provided by Dr. Rena Hall, none of this would have been possible. She had the vision to see that this partnership was possible and necessary to help our students receive the best possible education. Her professionalism, candor, and effective planning helped to align our efforts to ensure a seamless implementation. Also, she designed and facilitated high-quality, innovative, and engaging professional development training sessions that provided the tools and strategies for our teachers to fully understand all of the components of the Read to Succeed Program.

Rena's warmth and ability to relate to others created a warm and cohesive training environment, which generated an excitement about the program. With effective implementation, exceptional professional development, and a genuine desire to provide our students with an exceptional education through Napier's RTS program, our students have realized an immediate impact. The students' achievement scores have increased tremendously when compared to previous years. They have experienced more social and emotional support and have the skill set to self-regulate their behavior.

The parents feel a part of the process and empowered to make a difference in the lives of their children. All of these results will ultimately help to close the achievement gap that currently exists at Napier. None of this would have been possible without the foresight and expertise of Dr. Hall. She is simply amazing.

Dr. Watechia Lawless
Assistant Principal
Napier Enhanced Option School
Nashville, Tennessee

Bibliography

American Productivity and Quality Center (2014). "Building strong management capabilities processes." Retrieved November 11, 2014 from http://www.qualitydigest.com/read/content_by_author/26216#.

Annenberg Institute for School Reform (2014). "Professional learning communities." Retrieved December 10, 2014 from http://www.annenberginstitute.org/pdf/proflearning.pdf.

Ashwell, K (2012). *The Brain Book*. Buffalo, NY: Firefly Books.
Barr, K., Simmons, B., and Zarrow, J. (2003). "School coaching in context: A case study in capacity building." Paper presented at the American Educational Research Association annual meeting, Chicago.

Bessell, I. (2012). "Understanding motivation: An effective tool for managers." University of Florida, IFAS Extension.
Boston Consulting Group (2014). "Teachers know best: Teachers' views on professional development." Bill & Melinda Gates Foundation.

Christensen, K. (2010). "Creating and sustaining a successful professional development program." Moraine Valley Community College Center for Teaching & Learning.

Darling-Hammond, L., and McLaughlin, M. (1995). "Policies that support professional development in an era of reform." *Phi Delta Kappan* 76(8), 597–604.

DeMonte, J. (2013). "High-quality professional development for teachers: Supporting teacher training to improve student learning." Center for American Progress.

Dixon, J. (2014) "5 fresh ways to keep professional development engaging." Retrieved on January 6, 2015 from http://www.eschoolnews.com/2014/01/14/professional-development-engaging-407/.

Elmore, L.(1997). "Investing in teacher learning: Staff development and instructional improvement in community school district #2, New York City." Retrieved December 15, 2014 from http://www.eric.ed.gov/fulltext/ED416203.pdf.

Farina, C.(2014). "A Handbook of Professional Learning: Research, Resources, and Strategies for Implementation." NYC Department of Education.

Fullan, M.(2000). *Leading in a culture of change.* New York: Teachers College Press.

Fullan, M. (1991). *The New meaning of educational change.* New York: Teachers College Press.

Gardner, H. (2010). "Multiple intelligences." Retrieved November 12, 2014 from http://www.howardgardner.com/MI/mi.html.

Gordon, A. (2004). *Beginnings and beyond.* New York: Thompson Learning.

Griffith University (2014). "Principles to promote excellence in learning and teaching." Retrieved November 11, 2014 from http://www.griffith.edu.au/__data/assets/pdf_file/0006/120201/PrinciplesLandT.pdf.

Gulamhussein, A. (2013). "Teaching the teachers: Effective professional development in an era of high stakes accountability." Center for Public Education. Retrieved December 12, 2014 from htpps://www.centerforpubliceducation.org.

Guskey, T. (2002). "Does it make a difference? Evaluating professional development." *Redesigning Professional Development*, 59(6), 45-51.

Haslam, M. B. (2008). "Maryland Teacher Professional Development Guide." Harford County Public Schools.

Haslam, M. Bruce. "Teacher Professional Development Evaluation Guide." Washington DC: National Staff Development Council, 2010. www.nsdc.org.

Huffman, K. (2011). "Personal communication and interview." Imel, S. (2015). "Guidelines for working with adult learners: Creating an adult learning environment." 2015. Retrieved January 12, 2015 from ERIC Clearinghouse on Adult Learners (ERIC Digest No. 77).

Ischinger, B. (2009). "Creating effective teaching and learning environments." France: Teaching and Learning International Survey.

King's Daughters Child Development Center. (2014). Coaching Images, Madison, TN.

Knowles, M. (2014). "The adult learning theory: Andragogy." 2014. Retrieved December 1, 2014 from http://elearningindustry.com/the-adult-learning-theory-andragogy-of-malcolm-knowles.

Llopos, G. (2014). "The top 9 things that ultimately motivate employees to achieve." 2014. Retrieved from http://www.forbes.com/sites/glennllopis/2012/06/04/top-9-things-that-ultimately-motivate-employees-to-achieve/.

Lyons, C. and Pinnell, G (2001). *Systems for change in literacy education: A guide to professional development.* Portsmouth, NH: Heinemann.

Miller, E. (1995). "The old model of staff development survives in a world where everything else has changed." *The Harvard Education Letter* 11(1), 1–3.

Monaco, E. (2007). "Reviewing the evidence on how teacher professional development affects student achievement." Regional Educational Laboratory, 33.

Nagel, D. (2013). "Effective teacher professional development crucial to common core." Retrieved December 20, 2014, from http://cotsen.org/effective-teacher-professional-development-crucial-to-common-core.

National Staff Development Council. (2009). "Standards for staff development." Oxford: OH.

National Staff Development Council. (2001). "Standards for staff development." Oxford: OH.

Neufeld, B., and Roper, D. (2003). *Coaching: A strategy for developing instructional capacity ,promises, and practicalities.* Washington, DC, and Providence, RI: Aspen Institute Program on Education.

O'Day, J. (2002). "Complexity, Accountability, and School Improvement." *Harvard Educational Review*, 72(3), 293-329.

Pleasant, C. (2013). "Personal Communication."

Research Starters. (2015). "Professional & staff development opportunities. Retrieved February 17, 2015 from http://www.enotes.com/research-starters/professional-staff-development-opportunities#research-starter-research-starter.

Roy, P. (2013). "School-based professional learning: Managing change." *LearningForward.*

Sciarra, D., and Dorsey A. (2003). *Developing and administering a child care center.* NY: Thompson Learning.

Small, G., and Vorgan, G. (2008). *iBrain; Surviving the technological alteration of the modern mind.* New York: HarperCollins.

Sousa, D. (2009). "Brain-friendly learning for teachers." Association for Supervision and Curriculum Development, 66.

Strahl, B (2015)." Implementing best practice" requires a change strategy. Retrieved January 2, 2015 from: http://www.tapartnership.org/newsletter/archives/201206_OrganizationalDev.pdf.

Tate, M. (2007). Shouting won't grow dendrites: *20 techniques for managing a brain-compatible classroom.* CA: Corwin.

Teal Center Staff. (2011). "Adult learning theories. Teaching excellence in adult literacy fact sheet, 11."

Turchi, L. (2002). "The impact of accountability on the professional development of teachers: Preliminary evidence from case studies in six southern states." The Southeast Center for Teaching Quality.

United Way of Metropolitan Nashville. (2014). "Read to Succeed Program.

University of Oklahoma. (2011). "Coaching procedures." Retrieved October 2, 2014 from http://www.universityofoklahoma.edu.

University of Virginia. (2014). "Professional development." Retrieved December 20, 2014 from http://www.businessdictionary.com/definition/professional-development.html.

Zarrow, J. (2014). "5 strategies for better teacher professional development." 2014. Retrieved December 13, 2014 from http://www.teachthought.com/teaching/5-strategies-better-teacher-professional-development.

www.ingramcontent.com/pod-product-compliance
Lightning Source LLC
Chambersburg PA
CBHW042056290426
44112CB00001B/1